AMAZING
CRICKET
FACTS

AMAZING CRICKET FACTS

BY NICK CALLOW

All facts and figures are correct as of November 2004.

With thanks for their invaluable assistance to Olly Derbyshire, Nick Johnson, Dean Wilson, Simon Felstein and Hayters Teamwork Sports Agency

First published in Great Britain in 2005 by
Virgin Books Ltd
Thames Wharf Studios
Rainville Road
London
W6 9HA

ISBN 0 7535 1070 7

Typeset by Phoenix Photosetting, Chatham, Kent
Printed and bound in Great Britain by
Bookmarque Ltd

Contents

CONTENTS

In Your Dreams 175
Left-Handed Fantasy XI. The Tallest XI. The Smallest XI.
Fattest XI.

No Ball 185
Funny Old Name. Relative Success. Bad Cricket
Excuses. On The Head (Cricket Books). Famous Grounds.
One Club Wonders. Trivia

Foreword by Angus Fraser

In nearly twenty years as a professional cricketer I have seen and heard plenty of stories and tales that help to make the game as special as it is.

From the great W G Grace refusing to walk even when out to David Boon's ability to knock back a beer or fifty in a single flight to England, cricket has a whole host of quirks and oddities that I'm sure you will enjoy reading about in this book.

Even if cricket didn't have so many characters in the game, it would still have the ability to grab your attention with some eye-catching facts and figures from over a hundred years of competition.

Cricket takes its statistics very seriously, and rightly so, since they are the backbone of the game and allow everyone from commentator to regular punter to compare teams and players at a glance and discover just who the all-time greats of the game are.

I discovered just how hard international cricket was during my stint as an England player, so when you look at the achievements of some of the players within this book, you can believe me when I tell you they can't have been easy. Scoring a hundred, or taking five wickets, is a tremendous accomplishment in any era and takes some doing, but perhaps it is the efforts of the team to create winning streaks and series wins that provide the most impressive details.

By the time you've finished this book, you'll know a little more about the good and the great of the game, plus you'll be able to wow your mates with some unbelievable facts.

I hope you enjoy it.

HOWZAT!

Dazzling Debuts

Michael Clarke (Australia) 151: October 2004, Bangalore.
Twenty-three-year-old Clarke's dashing 151 in the first Test of the
Border Gavaskar Trophy included four huge sixes against the
deadly spin of Anil Kumble and Harbhajan Singh.

Andrew Strauss (England) 112 & 83: May 2004, Lord's.
Andrew Strauss got his opportunity at Test level thanks to an
injury to skipper Michael Vaughan. The Middlesex captain proved
his worth with a calm 112 in the first innings before setting up
victory in the second with 83 before being run-out by the retiring
Nasser Hussain.

Jacques Rudolph (South Africa) 222: April 2003, Chittagong.
With an unbeaten 222 in his debut Test innings, Jacques Rudolph
vindicated those who believed that he was a victim of reverse
discrimination in South African cricket. Twice he was in line for his
Test debut, and twice politics intervened. His first international

experience came during the unofficial match against India at
Centurion, in 2001–02, in the aftermath of the Mike Denness
affair. Two months later his selection to face Australia at Sydney
was reversed by the UCB President Percy Sonn on the grounds of
racial discrimination.

Lance Klusener (South Africa) 8 for 64: November 1996, Kolkata.
Already losing the series 1–0, South Africa needed a win to save
the series. With Allan Donald sidelined, 25-year-old Lance
Klusener shrugged off the horrors of his first innings yips to bowl
India out with figures of eight wickets for 64 runs.

Sourav Ganguly (India) 131 runs & 3 for 54: June 1996, Lord's.
Sourav Ganguly announced himself to the cricket world with two
centuries in his first two Test innings. He also chipped in with three
wickets on his debut and was decorated as India's Man of the
Series as the tourists were defeated 1–0. In April 2004, Ganguly
became India's most successful captain ever when he surpassed
Mohammad Azharuddin's tally of fourteen Test victories.

Dominic Cork (England) 7 for 43: June 1995, Lord's.
Dominic Cork ignited this Test series by destroying the West
Indies' second innings with a day of irresistible, away-swing
bowling. His figures of 7 for 43 were the best produced by an
England player on his debut and secured England's first victory
over the West Indies, at Lord's, for 38 years.

Graham Thorpe (England) 114: July 1993, Trent Bridge.
Graham Thorpe fulfilled his childhood dream by scoring a debut
century in an Ashes Test. Unfortunately, for England, Thorpe's

unbeaten 114 did little to turn the series around, England eventually losing 4–1 to a touring squad that included Shane Warne for the first time.

Mark Waugh (Australia) 138: January 1991, Adelaide.
The Australian's sterling 138 against England was the first of twenty elegant centuries from the tall stroke-maker. Waugh's promotion to the Test arena came at the expense of older brother Steve, yet this did little to disturb the concentration, grace, and panache of his first Test knock.

Narendra Hirwani (India) 16 for 136: January 1988, Madras.
Narendra Hirwani's Test career started with a bang, taking a record sixteen wickets in his debut Test. Hirwani followed that up with twenty more in his next three Tests but his career went relentlessly downhill from there, as he played out his career in domestic cricket where he never looked like repeating his one short-lived flirtation with greatness.

Mohammad Azharuddin (India) 110: December 1984, Kolkata.
The Indian's 110 runs on his debut were followed by two further centuries in the following two Tests, a feat yet to be repeated. Azhar joined the Indian team as they were locked at 1–1 in a fiercely contested series with England. Surprisingly, Azharuddin's form failed to inspire his new team-mates, as England went on to win the series 2–1.

Gordon Greenidge (West Indies) 93 & 107: November 1974, Bangalore.
Gordon Greenidge's debut contribution of 93 and 107 won West

Indies the first Test of a thrilling series that they would eventually win 3–2. Greenidge became one of the most powerful and prolific opening batsmen ever to play the game.

Lawrence Rowe (West Indies) 214 & 100*: February 1972, Jamaica.
Lawrence Rowe's average after his debut at his home ground, Sabina Park, stood at 314. Rowe's fairytale debut against New Zealand (214 and 100*) was blighted only by his allergy to grass that had the usually composed right-hander in a sneezing fit during his lengthy time at the crease.

* = not out

Famous for Fifteen Minutes

'I'm a deeply superficial person,' was Andy Warhol's less remembered quote. Some cricketers enjoy long and illustrious careers, others are in the spotlight for a comparatively short spell and then fade away, never to be heard of again. These are the cricketers who had just a brief brush with fame.

Bob Massie The Aussie fast-medium swing bowler made one of the most startling debuts in Test history. At Lord's in 1972, Massie swung the ball with devastating effect, taking eight wickets in each innings. His figures of 16 for 137 stood as a record for a Test debutant for fifteen years. But Massie failed to live up to his early promise, playing only five more Tests.

Gary Gilmour The Aussie paceman took 6 for 14 in the 1975 World Cup semi-final against England and 5 for 48 in the final against the West Indies. He followed that up with figures of 9 for 157 in the third Test at Headingley. But he was never the same again as injury problems and a loss of form took their toll.

Collis King He made his name in the final of the 1979 World Cup. The West Indies were struggling on 99 for 4 when he joined Viv Richards. In a fine display of batting, King made 86 from 66 balls, adding 139 with Richards in just 21 overs to put the match beyond England's reach. He was never able to reach such dizzy heights again in his career.

Laxman Sivaramakrishnan The Indian leg spinner won a Test match for India before his nineteenth birthday with 12 for 181 runs against England at Bombay in 1984–85. He was named Man of the Series after taking 23 wickets. Later that year, he played a key role as the Indian One-Day squad won the World Championship of Cricket in Australia. However, it was not long before Sivaramakrishnan's career went into freefall.

Richard Ellison After making his Test debut against the West Indies in 1984, Ellison was recalled to face Australia at Edgbaston the following year. The swing bowler claimed ten wickets in the match, with Allan Border among his victims. But he was never able to repeat those heroics on the international stage and he retired at the age of 33.

Matthew Elliott The left-handed opener was the star of Australia's 1997 Ashes success in England. He compiled 566 runs in the series, hitting centuries at Lord's and Headingley. Elliott was expected to be the lynchpin of the Australia side, but he struggled for form and lost his place. The reserved Victorian was rumoured to have had trouble fitting in with the dressing-room culture.

Eddo Brandes Probably the world's most famous chicken farmer, the Zimbabwean bowled superbly in the One-Day internationals against England in 1996–97. He claimed a hat-trick in the third match, bowling ten overs without a break and taking five wickets to give Zimbabwe victory. His fitness record was poor, however, and that proved to be the high point of his career.

Own Goals

They all go out to the centre of the pitch with the aim of coming back a match-winning hero. But some poor players will be remembered for all the wrong reasons. These are the players who reached for the stars, but ended up looking a wee bit silly.

Scott Boswell – Cheltenham and Gloucester Trophy Final 2001
The Leicestershire medium-paced bowler will be remembered for all the wrong reasons, as his two-over spell at the home of cricket was an exemplary display of self-destruction, costing 23 runs and featuring nine wides, eight in the second over, five in succession. His team failed to recover and Somerset went on to record a 41-run victory.

Inzaman-Ul-Haq – 2003 World Cup

Inzy's explosive batting has been the hallmark of a talented
Pakistan side for the past decade. However, the 2003 World Cup
was not the finest hour for the fourth highest One-Day scorer in
history. Pakistan's early exit had much to do with his spectacular
run of scores: 6,4,0,0,3 that included a golden duck against
England and a second-ball 0 against cricketing 'giants' The
Netherlands.

Chris Read – Second Test v New Zealand, 1999

The trouble with playing world-class opponents is that they have
the ability to make you look silly. Chris Cairns is a master of
variation, boasting the ability to bowl a collection of swingers,
slower balls and yorkers at will, and he put a bit of everything into
the delivery that made Chris Read try and duck a ball that pitched
on his bootlaces, bowling him for 0.

Dennis Lillee and Rodney Marsh – Fourth Test v England, 1981

At close of play on Day Three, Australia were firmly in control,
and the bookies placed England at 500–1 to win. Whether it was a
case of Australian showboating or just the lure of the impossible
wager, but Marsh and Lillee placed £10 each on a Pommie victory,
no doubt thinking 'what's the worst that can happen?' Ten
thousand pounds of embarrassment, that's what.

Fanie de Villiers – Third Test v England, 1994

De Villiers' decision to bounce England no.11 and ferocious fast
bowler Devon Malcolm must rank as one of the most counter-
productive in the history of the game. After the ball had removed
the badge from Malcolm's helmet, South African short leg Gary

HOWZAT!

Kirsten heard Devon utter the famous line: 'You guys are history.'
True to his word, Malcolm produced a devastating spell of 9 for
57 in just 99 balls, knocking Jonty Rhodes off his feet and squaring
the series in the process.

West Indies v Ireland, 1969

Fielding a line up that included team manager Clyde Walcott, the
world's greatest cricketing side were humbled at Sion Fields.
Maybe the West Indies took their eye off the ball in this contest,
being skittled out for just 25 in their first innings, Irish bowler
Goodwin took six wickets for just five runs. Walcott couldn't take
too much of the blame however, posting the second highest score
of six.

Brett Lee – Fourth Test v India, 2001

After bowling 29 no balls in two inauspicious displays, Lee's form
going into the Fourth Test could be described as patchy at best. At
the Sydney Cricket Ground the paceman outdid himself, sending
down no fewer than 24 no balls, two of which would have
otherwise resulted in the dismissal of Indian openers Akash
Chopra and Virender Sehwag.

Steve Waugh – Second Test v India, 2001

Responding to Australia's 1st innings score of 445, India stumbled
to 171 all out with V V S Laxman contributing a classy 59. Keen to
press home the advantage Waugh invited Laxman and co back to
the crease, and on day three he had to watch the Indians plunder
335 runs without offering a single chance to any of the nine
bowlers he employed. Laxman was finally dismissed on 281, and
Ganguly declared on 657 for 7. Fatigued by two and a half days

under the Indian sun, the Aussies capitulated to 212 all out, losing the game by 171 runs.

Sri Lanka – ICC Champions Trophy Final v Pakistan, 2001

Sanath Jaysuria provides a cautionary tale for any teams who place style over substance. Following defeat to Pakistan, the Sri Lankan captain didn't rely on the usual excuses such as umpiring or pitch conditions, but instead pointed the finger at the team tailor. 'We had to add extensions to the trousers and the shirts looked more like tight-fitting women's blouses.' The kits were subsequently altered and made bigger.

Herschelle Gibbs – World Cup Super Six Stage v Australia, 1999

Known as the man who dropped the World Cup, Gibbs spilled an easy chance from Australian captain Steve Waugh after starting his celebrations prematurely. Waugh, at that stage on 56, went on to finish on 120 not out. Australia won the game by five wickets and progressed from the tied semi-final between the two sides by virtue of countback. Reflecting on his clanger, Gibbs said: 'In quiet moments, my mind goes back to what happened and I break out in a cold sweat. I'm still suffering from flashbacks which send shivers down my spine.'

Ian Healy – Third Test v West Indies 1999

Australia were crushing teams left, right and centre, while the Windies were playing on the back of a 5–0 thrashing at the hands of South Africa. The series is square at 1–1 and Australia are in control until a demolition job by Courtney Walsh, who took 5 for 39, bowls them out for just 146, leaving 311 for victory. The West Indies shouldn't have had a prayer, but enter Brian Lara and it was game on.

HOWZAT!

With only two wickets to take and with Curtly Ambrose at the other end, Jason Gillespie gets the all important edge off Lara's bat and the record-breaking wicket-keeper Ian Healy just has to claim the simple chance. He somehow drops it, the Windies win and Lara is the hero yet again.

Bizarre Merchandise

Like many sporting fans, followers of cricket love to collect the tat and memorabilia that surround the game. Here are a few of some of cricket's more unusual items that one can buy.

A large fake moustache became an important fashion accessory for cricket followers around the world between 1985 and 1994. Merv 'the Swerve' Hughes became a legend everywhere he played with his shaven head, big moustache, snarling deliveries and elaborate limbering up exercises.

The Edgbaston souvenir shop produced a collector's item in 2003 when a manufacturer's error produced a batch of £4 mugs celebrating Ashley Giles as 'The King of Spain'. The errant 'A' was corrected with one original presented to His Majesty Ashley Giles at his Warwickshire testimonial.

Made famous in the 1970s and 80s by Richard Hadlee, Martin Crowe and co., New Zealand's Tan and Brown kit enjoyed a revival with Kiwi fans when the black caps toured England in the summer of 2004.

The eccentricities of English cricket are still glaringly on view in the Long Room at Lord's. The MCC's egg-and-bacon stripes are no longer seen only on ties and hats but also on blazers.

England's Barmy Army have been promoting British class around the globe since their formation in 1995. The sight of two thousand drunk men wearing fake breasts…!

A 'Cricket Australia' barbeque set is currently selling on e-bay for the bargain price of AUS $55.

For the most dedicated Shane Warne fan a personalised Shane Warne souvenir number plate is available.

Twenty-cent Donald Bradman coins can be purchased from e-bay. The Aussie obsession with their legendary player continues.

Superstitions

Cricketers are a superstitious lot, as the following rituals illustrate …

England batsman **Marcus Trescothick** wears his gloves in the changing room after he is out.

Aussie **Steve Waugh** and Indian Test star **Sourav Ganguly** both have a red hanky tucked into their pockets when they are playing.

India batsman **Rahul Dravid** is careful about putting his right foot first on the ground.

HOWZAT!

India's **Nikhil Chopra** has to have the colour yellow or black splashed somewhere on his attire before he goes to play.

Legendary Indian opener **Sunil Gavaskar** always grounds his bat first before bringing his right foot into position, while taking guard.

Mohammad Azharuddin, the former India batsman, circled his head twice before taking strike.

India Test star **Kris Srikanth** used to sniffle his nose and saunter towards the square leg umpire after facing each delivery.

Pakistan great **Imran Khan** wore a 'tiger' T-shirt in the finals of the 1992 World Cup as a matter of superstition.

Aussie batting star **Mark Waugh** always raised his collar as he walked onto the field.

Sri Lanka's **Sanath Jayasuriya** goes through the elaborate ritual of touching all his cricket equipment before taking guard.

Indian Test star **Sachin Tendulkar** always puts his left pad on first.

West Indies all-rounder **Phil Simmons** always had a cross attached to his sweater.

Sri Lanka batsman **Roshan Mahanama** keeps touching his bat to his chin when he is batting.

Hidden Talents – Cricketers With Other Skills

Not all cricketers are one dimensional chaps. In fact, some of them have more about them than just the ability to throw, catch and hit a ball around a field.

Former Somerset player **Bill Alley**, who went on to become a first-class umpire, earned his living as a prize fighter in his younger days. He boasted an undefeated record.

Andy Caddick has no need to worry if the traffic gets too bad. The England Test star can always get airborne as he is a fully qualified helicopter pilot.

Former Derbyshire opener **Peter Gibbs** is a playwright who has written episodes of the popular ITV drama *Heartbeat*.

Eccentric ex-England wicketkeeper **Jack Russell** is a talented artist, painting a diverse range of subjects. The Jack Russell Art Gallery is situated in Chipping Sodbury, Gloucestershire.

Mark Butcher is a talented musician, playing the guitar. When his Surrey team-mate Ben Hollioake died in a car accident, Butcher wrote and recorded a tribute song called 'You're Never Gone', with proceeds from the sale of the CD going to charity.

Controversial former Hampshire, Sussex, Warwickshire and Surrey star **Ed Giddins** is a keen poker player and has appeared in some televised tournaments.

When he is not spinning a cricket ball, Kent's **Min Patel** can often be seen spinning discs as a DJ.

Don't upset Yorkshire and England bowler **Chris Silverwood** – he can look after himself as a black belt in karate.

HOWZAT!

Aussie bowler **Andy Bichel** is a mad-keen angler who loves a day on the water chasing anything from mackerel to flatties.

They've Got the Runs

Certainly the names that follow in these categories have got them big time. You just have to sit back and admire their achievements.

Most Test Runs

In a Game

1. Brian Lara (400)
Became the first man to reclaim the world Test batting record, when he hit an unbeaten 400 in April 2004 in a desperate bid to save West Indies from a home series whitewash in the final Test against England. The Trinidadian left-hander faced 582 deliveries at Antigua's Recreational Ground, hitting 43 fours and 4 sixes, but time ran out for the West Indies and they could only draw the Test.

2. Matthew Hayden (380)
Hayden beat Lara's initial highest Test innings total by pounding his way to 380 during the second day of Australia's first Test against

Zimbabwe in 2003. The left-handers' innings included 11 sixes and 38 fours from 437 balls in 622 minutes at the crease. He was finally caught by Stuart Carlisle off Trevor Gripper, but Australia eased home by an innings and 175 runs.

3. Brian Lara (375)

Same venue, same opposition, same result – only it was ten years earlier when Lara set his first record for an individual highest innings. During 766 minutes and 538 balls, Lara hit 375 runs, despite failing to convert any of his 45 boundaries into sixes. Jack Russell eventually caught him behind from an Andrew Caddick delivery.

4. Sir Gary Sobers (365)

The original West Indies batsman to hold the record for most runs in a Test innings, before Lara came to the forefront almost forty years later. The all-rounder, racked up an unbeaten 365 in the Third Test win over Pakistan in 1958. It was Sobers' first Test century.

5. Sir Len Hutton (364)

For nearly two decades, Len Hutton's innings of 364 for England against Australia in 1938 was the highest score for a batsman in Test cricket. In helping England reach a total of 903 for 7, Hutton spent a mammoth thirteen hours, seventeen minutes at the crease, and recorded what turned out to be England's 100th century against Australia. The match was drawn, but across the country church bells pealed 364 times to honour his achievement.

6. Sanath Jayasuriya (340)

Jayasuriya has proven he is a batsman capable of producing huge cricket totals in both ODI and Test cricket, as his presence in both top tens demonstrates. His biggest Test run haul came in the 1997 first Test stalemate against India where he chalked up 340, before being beaten by Sourav Ganguly's catch off Rajesh Chauhan's bowling, 799 minutes and 578 balls after first entering the crease.

7. Hanif Mohammad (337)

The 'Little Master's' marathon innings of sixteen hours and ten minutes produced a then-record 337 runs, after Pakistan were forced to follow on against the West Indies in the opening Test of the series at Bridgetown. Thanks to Mohammad's endurance the six-day Test was drawn. However, only 40 days later, in the third Test of that same series, Gary Sobers surpassed his record.

8. Wally Hammond (336)

In contrast to Mohammad, Hammond took only 318 minutes to make his mark on the highest run Test innings chart. He scored a record breaking 336 not out, including a whopping 34 fours and 10 sixes, against New Zealand as England romped towards 548 for 7 before declaring. However, rain denied England the chance of victory soon after the start of the third day.

9. Sir Donald Bradman (334)

Along with Brian Lara, Bradman is the only other player to score two triple Test centuries in international cricket. His greatest haul came against England at Headingley on 12 July 1930. He made 334, scoring 309 of those runs on the opening day of the third

Test, which ended all square, on his first tour of England with the Australian side.

10. Mark Taylor (334)

Taylor equalled Bradman and with it Australia's then highest innings by a single batsman when he hit an unbeaten 334 in the second Test draw with Pakistan in October 1998. The batting opener played out 720 minutes at the crease, facing 564 balls.

11. Chris Wishart (172*)

Wishart hit a commanding 172 not out to set up an 86-run victory for World Cup hosts Zimbabwe over Namibia in a rain-curtailed Group A match in 2003. Wishart played the entire 191 minutes of Zimbabwe's innings facing 151 balls and hitting 3 sixes from his 21 boundaries.

* = not out

In a Season

1. Sir Viv Richards

It is more than 25 years since Sir Viv scored 1,710 runs in eleven Tests in 1976, and still no one has come within 200 runs of his monumental total. With 5 fifties, 5 tons, and 2 double tons, he punished Australian, Indian and English bowlers alike, at an average of 90.00 without recording a single not out.

2. Ricky Ponting

The Australian captain was in imperious form in 2003, and although off to a bad start with a seven and an eleven in the 'dead' fifth Test against England at the start of the year, scored 1,503 runs in 18 innings, at an average of 100.20. After scoring two centuries and a double ton in the Caribbean, Ponting faced Bangladesh and Zimbabwe before recording 242 and 257 in back-to-back Tests against India.

3. Michael Vaughan

Having spent a couple of years on the fringes of the England team, Vaughan cemented his place in the side with some sparkling batting performances in 2002. A modest 131 runs in three Tests in New Zealand was followed by 900 runs in seven home Tests against Sri Lanka and India, a prelude to an incredible series in Australia, where he became the first visiting batsman for 32 years to top 600 runs, 450 of which came in 2002 as part of his 1,481 run total for the year.

4. Sunil Gavaskar

The Indian side had a very busy 1979 playing seventeen Test matches, and Gavaskar spent more time out in the middle than any of his team-mates as he racked up 1,407 runs from 26 innings, against the West Indies, England, Australia, and Pakistan, the highest score coming in the fourth Test in England with 221 in the second innings at the Oval, as the tourists ran out of time chasing 438 to win.

5. Sachin Tendulkar

The Indian batsman was at his dominant best in 2002 as he scored 1,392 runs from his 26 innings. Despite scoring 4 centuries and 5 fifties, Tendulkar also managed to record 3 ducks in 4 innings against the West Indies.

THEY'VE GOT THE RUNS

6. Matthew Hayden
By smashing 1,391 runs from 25 innings in 2001 Hayden broke Bob Simpson's Australian record for most Test runs in a calendar year. Including 549 runs on the tour to India, an Australian record for a three-match series, and consecutive scores of 131 and 138 against South Africa, it was a good year for the big Queenslander.

7. Gundappa Viswanath
'Vishy' got off to a fine start in 1979 with 124 out of 255 against the West Indies on a fiery, bouncy Madras wicket, which proved vital as India won the match, and continued his form throughout the year with four more tons and six half-centuries. In all, he scored 1,388 runs from 26 innings.

8. Bob Simpson
The Australian captain went into 1964 without a Test century to his name, but in the fourth Test at Old Trafford he finally made his way into three figures, and he didn't stop there, claiming 311 before being caught behind. Simmo added a ton in each innings in the first Test against Pakistan to finish the year with 1,381 runs from 26 innings.

9. Dennis Amiss
Opening partner of Geoffrey Boycott, the strong right hander turned half of his fifties in Test cricket into three-figure scores, and in 1974 he had an even better return, only stopping short of the century three times after reaching fifty. The pick of his 5 tons was a match saving 262 not out in Kingston, as he scored 1,379 runs in the calendar year.

10. Rahul Dravid

Dravid was at the height of his powers in 2002 as he recorded centuries in four consecutive innings, with 115, 148, and 217 coming against England and 100 not out achieved against the West Indies before he retired hurt. In total he scored 1,357 runs against Zimbabwe and West Indies at home, and West Indies, England, and New Zealand on tour.

In a Career

Looking at the top run scorers of all time reads like a 'Who's Who' of modern batting. As in football, the numbers never lie. The batsmen's averages appear in brackets.

1. Allan Border – Australia

Took over the captaincy of a struggling Australian side and lifted them almost single-handedly to the top of the Test match pile, leading the way with his mental and physical tenacity, racking up 11,174 (50.56) runs in 156 matches.

2. Steve Waugh – Australia

Another tough Aussie skipper, Waugh broke into Test match cricket aged twenty, before losing his place to his twin brother Mark. Steve learned from the setback, and came back with more mature batting performances that saw him score 10,927 (51.06) runs in his 168 Tests.

3. Sunil Gavaskar – India

The first man to score 10,000 runs in Tests, 'Sunny' is one of the finest opening batsmen of all time. He has still scored more Test match tons than any other player – there are 34 centuries among his 10,122 (51.12) runs in 125 matches.

4. Brian Lara – West Indies
One of the most aesthetically pleasing batsmen of all time, 'The Prince' has always enjoyed recording big scores and is the only man to claim the highest Test score twice with his 375 in 1994 and his 400 not out in 2004 proving he's not finished yet, with 10,094 (52.84) runs in 112 Tests to date.

5. Sachin Tendulkar – India
Since making his Test debut aged sixteen, Tendulkar has scored 9,470 (57.39) runs in his 114 matches. Tipped by Sunil Gavaskar to be the first man to break the 15,000 run barrier, and compared favourably to Bradman, by the Don himself.

6. Graham Gooch – England
Missed three years of Test match cricket whilst in his prime, for leading the first rebel tour of South Africa, Gooch would surely have been the first Englishman to break the 10,000-run mark if not for his self-inflicted hiatus. He scored 8,900 (42.58) runs in 118 Tests.

7. Javed Miandad – Pakistan
Miandad scored six Test centuries before his 22nd birthday, and continued to notch up big scores in the International arena until he was 36, scoring 8,832 (52.57) runs in 124 matches.

8. Viv Richards – West Indies
The most intimidating batting presence cricket has known, he never lost a series as captain of the West Indies, and his

monumental total of 8,540 (50.23) runs, in his 121 Tests, went a long way to preserve that remarkable statistic.

9. Alec Stewart – England
Arguably the finest batting wicket-keeper Test cricket has seen, Stewart came into the England side relatively late as a spritely 27-year-old, but his fitness and athleticism saw him go on to play more Tests than any other Englishman. He scored 8,463 (39.54) in 133 matches.

10. David Gower – England
Although he was an elegant stroke-playing opener who was great to watch, the old school pedants say he fell short of his potential, due to a combination of lazy footwork and a lack of concentration. It made him more interesting to watch, though, and he still scored a remarkable 8,231 (44.25) runs in 117 matches.

Most One-Day Runs

In a Game

1. Saeed Anwar (194)
The Pakistan batsman chalked up 194 runs from 146 balls in 1997, to claim the most runs ever scored by a single batsman in a One-Day international. It also helped his country to a 35-run win against India. Anwar hit 22 fours and 5 sixes on the way to his mammoth total, lasting 3 hours and 26 minutes before being caught by Sourav Ganguly off Sachin Tendulkar's bowling.

THEY'VE GOT THE RUNS

2. Sanath Jayasuriya (189)
The architect of Sri Lanka's Coca-Cola Champions Trophy triumph over India in 2000. Jayasuriya rescued an innings that was dipping into the doldrums with a breathtaking 189 from just 161 balls, including 25 boundaries, 4 of which were sixes, before eventually being stumped out.

3. Viv Richards (189)
Held the record for thirteen years before Anwar, with an unbeaten 189 off 170 balls, against England at Old Trafford in 1984. He scored 21 fours and 5 sixes, as the West Indies roared to a 104-run victory.

4. Gary Kirsten (188)
South Africa thrashed United Arab Emirates by 169 runs in the 1996 World Cup. However, despite remaining unbeaten, Kirsten fell a solitary run short of equalling Richards' then record, totting up a score of 188.

5. Sachin Tendulkar (186*)
In 1999, India's Tendulkar marked his 24th One-Day international century with his highest One-Day score to date. He finished not out on a scintillating 186 as India overcame New Zealand by 174 runs.

6. Sourav Ganguly (183)
Tendulkar's compatriot Ganguly hit 183 runs, as India romped to a 157-run victory in a 1999 World Cup Group match, to the dismay of the then reigning champions, Sri Lanka, who caught him out too late in the innings to salvage the match. Ganguly's 210-minute spell at the crease yielded 17 fours and 7 sixes.

7. Viv Richards (181)
The West Indies' greatest One-Day batsman hit another huge total at the expense of the Sri Lankans at Sri Lanka's National Stadium, in 1987. 'King Viv' was caught on 181 runs off 127 balls, as the Windies stormed past their counterparts by 191 runs.

8. Kapil Dev (175*)
India's 60-over World Cup Group B win over Zimbabwe saw Dev notch up an unbeaten 175 from 138 deliveries. Dev smashed 22 boundaries, including 6 sixes in the 31-run success.

9. Mark Waugh (173)
Less than a day before he faced cricket's anti-corruption investigators over his alleged involvement with illegal Indian bookmakers, Waugh belted the highest One-Day score by an Australian of 173 to give his country a 39-run win over the West Indies, in 2001.

10. Adam Gilchrist (172)
Gilchrist's 172 run haul, in 2004, set Australia on their way to the highest ODI total reached on Australian soil – 7 for 344. However, he failed to last to the end of the innings, being bowled swiping at a straight ball from Zimbabwe's Sean Ervine in the 46th over, one run short of fellow countryman Mark Waugh's 173. Australia won the One-Dayer by 148 runs.

11. Chris Wishart (172*)
Wishart hit a commanding 172 not out to set up an 86-run victory for World Cup hosts Zimbabwe over Namibia in a rain-curtailed Group A match in 2003. Wishart played the entire 191 minutes of

Zimbabwe's innings facing 151 balls and hitting 3 sixes from his 21 boundaries.

In a Season

The limited overs version of cricket has not limited the best players from racketing up some impressive scores. For some unknown reason, batsmen from one country in particular seem to excel here. Many Indians enjoy cricket, but their batsmen seem really to love the One-Day version of the game as this section charting the players with the most runs from One-Day games in a calendar year illustrates.

1. Sachin Tendulkar
He is the all-time top scorer in ODI cricket, the Indian legend peaked in 1998 with 1,894 runs from 33 innings, at an impressive average of 65.31. The Little Master scored 7 fifties, and 9 tons, the pick of which were back-to-back scores of 143 and 134 against Australia to win the Coca-Cola Cup, in Sharjah.

2. Sourav Ganguly
India's most successful Test captain is also one of only two men – the other being Tendulkar – to have recorded more than 1,000 ODI runs in a calendar year five times. The most prolific of which was 1999, when Ganguly scored 1,767 from his 41 innings, at an average of 46.50.

3. Rahul Dravid
Dravid was very busy in 1999, playing 43 One-Day internationals. He acted as wicket-keeper in six of them, averaging 60.40 in the

games in which he took responsibility with the gloves compared to 46.34 for the year as a whole, in which he scored 1,761 runs.

4. Sachin Tendulkar

Indian batsmen's dominance of the modern One-Day game is made evident by Tendulkar completing a top four of men from the sub-continent. It was a case of all or nothing for the Indian talisman as he scored 6 centuries, 9 fifties, and was out 8 times in single figures on his way to 1,611 runs for the year.

5. Saeed Anwar

The year before his ODI record score of 194, Anwar was at his most prolific in the shorter form of the game, scoring 1,595 in his 36 innings. The opener was at his best in the Champions Trophy in Sharjah where he guided Pakistan to victories over New Zealand and Sri Lanka with consecutive unbeaten centuries of 104* and 112*.

6. Sourav Ganguly

By scoring 1,579 ODI runs in 2000, Ganguly became the first man to score more than 1,000 runs in four consecutive years in One-Dayers. With 7 tons and 6 half-centuries, Ganguly also carried his bat four times with scores of 105*, 135*, 141*, and 71*.

7. Mark Waugh

In late 1998, it became public knowledge that Waugh and his Australian team-mate Shane Warne had accepted money from an Indian bookmaker, but that low point in his career simply spurred him on and, in 1999, the Sydney-born batsman racked up 1,468 runs for the year, including some crucial runs in his country's World Cup win.

8. Gary Kirsten
In 2000, Kirsten went past 50 in 15 of his ODI innings, but he only converted two of those knocks into centuries. Despite this poor statistic, the Western Province opener scored 1,467 runs in 36 matches, breaking the South African record he set in 1996.

9. Gary Kirsten
South Africa's most consistent One-Day performer, Kirsten notched up 1442 runs in 1996 from just 29 games. The Cape Town-born batsman hit 4 half centuries and 6 tons, including unbeaten scores of 188, 115, 118, and 105.

10. Yousuf Youhana
One of the few Christians to play for Pakistan, the right-hander now dominates the middle order and, in 2002, he was in breathtaking form with 1,362 runs from 30 innings. A 129 Man-of-the-Match performance in the final of the Sharjah Cup against Sri Lanka was followed by a 125 against New Zealand in his next match. Later in the year, Youhana scored 317 unbeaten runs over three innings against Zimbabwe: 141*, 76* and 100*.

In a Career

1. Sachin Tendulkar (13,415)
Pint-sized Tendulkar has consistently produced the goods on the One-Day circuit for well over a decade, scoring more centuries than any other batsman, which probably goes someway to

explaining how he leads the all-time One-Day scoring charts by more than 3,000 runs, with a total of 13,415 from 330 innings.

2. Inzamam-Ul-Haq (10,192)

His burly physique means he may not be the greatest runner between the wickets, but he still remains one of the biggest and most devastating hitters in cricket. Having hit more half centuries than anyone else in the One-Day game, the 6" 2' right-hander averages 39.20 and has a total of 10,192 runs in 303 innings.

3. Sanath Jayasuriya (9,853)

In total the Sri Lankan skipper has rattled up 9,853 runs in 323 innings of One-Day cricket. The left-handed batsman was in sensational form in January 2003, scoring two tons and a 99 in ten days of action, and he also holds a particularly impressive scoring rate of 88.65 per 100 balls.

4. Sourav Ganguly (9,789)

Ganguly's One-Day batting record currently stands 9,789 runs from just 253 innings, averaging 42.01. His pairing with the destructive Sachin Tendulkar proved to be the most successful ODI opening partnership in history, surpassing the partnership of Gordon Greenidge and Desmond Haynes, with 5,308 in 116 innings together.

5. Mohammad Azharuddin (9,378)

Right-handed batsman 'Azhar' scored 9,378 runs in a career spanning sixteen years, between 1984 and 2000. He was called in to bat in 308 out of the 334 matches he played for India, failing to be dismissed 54 times and averaging 36.92.

THEY'VE GOT THE RUNS

6. Aravinda De Silva (9,284)

Lying sixth in the all-time one-day run scores, De Silva amassed 9,284 runs from 296 innings for Sri Lanka in a distinguished One-Day career, the highlight of which being the 1996 World Cup win in which De Silva hit an unbeaten century in the final, as well as picking up four Man-of-the- Match accolades during the tournament.

7. Brian Lara (8,921)

Renowned for his endeavours at Test level, as the current holder of the most runs in a Test innings, Lara has also proven rather useful with a bat in the One-Day game. He has hit 8,921 runs, averaging 42.28 in 237 innings.

8. Saeed Anwar (8,823)

The current holder of the highest individual score in a One-Day innings, with 194 against India in 1997, he has scored 8,823 runs at a high scoring rate of 80.60 every 100 balls. His average of 39.21 from 244 innings was helped greatly by his three consecutive centuries in 1982. Only three other batsmen have ever achieved such a feat in the One-Day arena.

9. Desmond Haynes (8,648)

Only recently overtaken by Lara as West Indies' highest ever One-Day international scorer, Haynes bagged 8,648 runs during his 238-game ODI career, at an average of 41.38 and a scoring rate of 63.09 per 100 balls.

10. Mark Waugh (8,500)

Possibly the greatest ODI batsman produced by Australia, who in turn are arguably the most successful One-Day country in the world, having won more World Cups than any other. Waugh hit three centuries in the 1996 World Cup and eventually got his hands on the trophy in 1999. He was the fifth batsman in the world to complete 8,000 runs in One-Day cricket before retiring in 2002 with One-Day stats of 8,500 runs in 236 innings, an average of 39.35.

SHARP SHOOTERS

The fastest Test centuries, in terms of the time taken, are as follows:

70 minutes: **Jack Gregory** for Australia v South Africa at Johannesburg, 1921–22.

75 minutes: **Gilbert Jessop** for England v Australia at The Oval, 1902.

78 minutes: **Richie Benaud** for Australia v West Indies at Kingston, 1954–55.

80 minutes: **Jimmy Sinclair** for South Africa v Australia at Cape Town, 1902–03.

81 minutes: **Sir Viv Richards** West Indies v England at St John's, 1985–86.

The fastest Test centuries, in terms of the number of balls received, are as follows:

56 balls: **Sir Viv Richards** for West Indies v England at St John's, 1985–86.

67 balls: **Jack Gregory** for Australia v South Africa at Johannesburg, 1921–22.

69 balls: **Shivnarine Chanderpaul** for West Indies v Australia at Georgetown, 2002–03.

71 balls: **Roy Fredericks** for West Indies v Australia at Perth, 1975–76.

74 balls: **Mohammad Azharuddin** for India v South Africa at Calcutta, 1996–97.

74 balls: **Majid Khan** for Pakistan v New Zealand at Karachi, 1976–77.

74 balls: **Kapil Dev** for India v Sri Lanka at Kanpur, 1986–87.

Best Openers

A successful opening partnership can lay the foundations for a good innings, hence the need for consistency at the top of the batting order. The following players have contributed many a solid performance to set their teams on the way to victory.

Jack Hobbs Known as 'The Master', Hobbs was cricket's most prolific batsman, hitting 61,237 first-class runs and 197 centuries. The Surrey and England legend also remains, at the age of 46, the oldest player to score a Test century.

Herbert Sutcliffe Combining courage with concentration, Sutcliffe was an artist of the dead bat and an uncompromising hooker of fast bowling. He scored over 50,000 runs at an average of 52 for Yorkshire and England.

Bill Lawry The Australian opener was a courageous batsman who withstood some fearsome deliveries. He was the success story of Richie Benaud's '61 side that retained the Ashes, scoring centuries at Lord's and Old Trafford to finish the series with an average of 52.5.

Geoff Boycott The Yorkshire and England legend was a dogged player, protecting his wicket as if his life depended on it. He saw his first task as scoring heavily enough to protect his teams against defeat and played attacking strokes sparingly. Boycott scored over 8,000 Test runs.

Sunil Gavaskar One of the greatest opening batsmen of all time, the Indian star boasted a near-perfect technique and had tremendous powers of concentration. He holds the record for the highest number of Test centuries, having reached the three-figure mark on 34 occasions.

Gordon Greenidge A massively destructive batsman who formed a prolific opening partnership with Desmond Haynes in the West Indies side, his unbeaten 214 at Lord's in 1984, to set up a nine-wicket win over England, is considered one of the great innings of all time.

Mike Atherton A gutsy, single-minded opener with a strong defensive technique, Atherton scored over 7,000 runs for England in 115 Tests. He captained his country on 54 occasions.

Matthew Hayden The tall Aussie has great mental and physical strength. Hayden has formed a prolific opening partnership with

Justin Langer. By the end of 2001 he had broken Bob Simpson's Australian record for most Test runs in a calendar year.

Fastest Victories

Since 1947, the following matches have been completed on the first day:

Derbyshire v Somerset, at Chesterfield, in 1947.
Lancashire v Sussex, at Manchester, in 1950.
Surrey v Warwickshire, at The Oval, in 1953.
Somerset v Lancashire, at Bath, in 1953.
Kent v Worcestershire, at Tunbridge Wells, in 1960.

The Keeper Has Scored!

(Centuries from Number 11s and Number 10s)

When a fielding side gets the opposition eight or nine wickets down, they can start to think that their job is done, and maybe think about their batting, or what they can do to pass the time back in the pavilion, but if you take your eyes off the game there's always a chance that the tail can earn some big runs to make you look very silly indeed.

Brian Hastings & Richard Collinge
Collinge has the highest Test score for a number eleven batsman, with his 68*, as part of the overall tenth-wicket Test record of 151, for New Zealand against Pakistan at Auckland in 1972–73.

Azhar Mahmood & Mushtaq Ahmed

The two Pakistan bowlers equalled the Test record tenth wicket partnership against South Africa at Rawalpindi in October 1997. Coming in at 206 for 6, Azhar Mahmood scored an unbeaten 128, as he put on 74 for the ninth wicket with Waqar Younis, and 151 for the tenth with Mushtaq Ahmed, 59.

Wasim Raja & Wasim Bari

The next highest tenth-wicket stand, was between two other Pakistanis, as Wasim Raja put on 133 with wicket-keeper Wasim Bari, 60 not out. Raja was in fine form as his second innings 71 followed his unbeaten 117 in the first innings.

Wilfred Rhodes & Frank Foster

The all-time English tenth wicket record stands at 130. The record was set by Wilfred Rhodes, 40*, and Frank Foster as England posted a match-winning total of 577 in the first Ashes Test, in 1903. 'Tip' Foster's 287 remains the highest score by a player in their first Test, and is still England's highest in Australia.

Ken Higgs & John Snow

Two runs short of the all-time English tenth-wicket record, Higgs, 63, and Snow, 59*, can console themselves with the knowledge that they still have the highest partnership in Tests between the ten and eleven in a Test side. Their tenth wicket stand of 128, was part of a dramatic turnaround as England went from 166–7 to 527 all out in the first innings against West Indies at The Oval in 1966.

Danny Morrison & Nathan Astle

In January 1996 New Zealand's final wicket of the second innings saved the first Test against England. By remaining unbeaten for nearly three hours Morrison and Astle's obdurate last wicket rally saved the Black Caps from certain defeat. Morrison came to the crease half an hour after lunch and faced exactly half of the 266 balls bowled at the pair, as they put on an unbeaten 106.

Walter Read

'W.W.' still holds the record score for a number ten in Test cricket with his 117 in England's first innings against Australia at The Oval in 1884. The home side only made 346, and had to follow on, but they batted out a draw comfortably.

Sir Viv Richards & Michael Holding

The West Indies were struggling on 166–9, before Holding joined Richards at the crease. The pair batted out the innings at Old Trafford in 1984 to put an extra 106 runs on the total of 272. Richards (189*) and Holding's (12*) partnership remains the highest tenth-wicket stand in One-Day international cricket, albeit a 55-over match.

* = Not Out

Most Centuries in Consecutive One-Day Internationals

Scoring a century is the name of the game for the world's best batsmen. That's all very well when you have days and days and days of a Test match, but not so easy when you have the limited overs of a One-Day International game. All of the guys have hit at least a couple of One-Day tons in a row.

Zaheer Abbas (Pakistan)

The Pakistan legend had an appetite for runs that saw him labelled as the Asian Bradman. He was the first man to score three consecutive One-Day hundreds, as his scores of 118, 105, and 113 secured a 3–1 series win over India in 1982–83, all of which came at the rate of more than a run every ball.

Saeed Anwar (Pakistan)

The record-breaking Pakistan batsman excels in the short form of the game. As well as making the highest score in a One-Dayer, Saeed scored tons in three consecutive ODIs at the 1993 Sharjah Cup against Sri Lanka and West Indies 107, 131, and 111. He has also scored back-to-back One-Day centuries on three other occasions: in the 1996 Sharjah Cup 104* against New Zealand and 112* against South Africa. In the 1999 World Cup he hit 103 against Zimbabwe and 113* against New Zealand, in England. In the ICC Knock-Out in Nairobi in 2000 Saeed scored 105* against Sri Lanka, and 104 against New Zealand.

Herschelle Gibbs (South Africa)

At the ICC Champions Trophy in Sri Lanka in 2002, Gibbs hit 116 to beat Kenya but his 166 before retiring hurt wasn't enough to beat India, and South Africa were out at the semi-final stage. In his next match he scored a match-winning 153 against Bangladesh, and Gibbs came close to making his own record of four in a row, as he hit an unbeaten 97 off 66 balls in the next match against the minnows.

Brian Lara (West Indies)

Throughout his long career the Prince of the Caribbean has always had big scores in him, and three times he has hit centuries in successive ODIs. In 1993 Lara scored 128 to beat South Africa almost single-handedly, and repeated the trick four days later with 111 not out. In Australia in 1997, the gifted leftie followed 102 against the hosts with an unbeaten 103 against Pakistan. Lara completed his third double in the 2003 World Cup against South Africa, scoring 116, five months after his 111 against Kenya.

Sanath Jayasuriya (Sri Lanka)
Sri Lanka's captain lead by example in 2003 as he struck back-to-back tons, 122 and 106, against Australia and England. Relieved of the captaincy, the gifted stroke player repeated the feat in the 2004 Asia Cup with 107* against Bangladesh and 130 against India.

Roy Dias (Sri Lanka)
The first man to score hundreds in consecutive ODIs, Dias hit big scores twice against India in 1982, with 102 and 121. But neither score was enough to take Sri Lanka to victory in Delhi or Bangalore.

Mark Greatbatch (New Zealand)
The only Kiwi to make three figures in successive One-Dayers, Greatbatch reached 102*, guiding the Black Caps to victory at Headingley, but his 111 at The Oval wasn't enough to beat England.

Mark Waugh (Australia)
Considering the Australian dominance of the short game in recent years, it is something of a surprise that no Aussie has scored back-to-back tons in One-Day internationals since Waugh in 1996. In the World Cup against Kenya, 130, and India, 126, he became only the third of his countrymen to achieve the feat after Geoff

'Swampy' Marsh (113 and 106* v WI, 1991), and Dean Jones (104 v ENG and 121 v PAK, 1987).

India's Big Four

India's current batting power is highlighted by the fact that **Sachin Tendulkar** (143 and 134 v AUS, 1998), **Rahul Dravid** (104* v KEN and 145 v SL, 1999), **Saurav Ganguly** (141* v SA and 117 v NZ, 2000), and **V V S Laxman** (106* v AUS and 131 v ZIM, 2000) have all hit centuries in successive One-Day innings, Virender Sehwag may feel a little left out.

David Gower (England)

The brilliant left-hander was the first Englishman to score tons in consecutive ODIs with 122 and 158 against New Zealand in 1983. His achievement has since been matched by six of his countrymen (see below):

Other batsmen to score consecutive One-Day centuries:

England – Graham Gooch (115 and 117* v AUS, 1985); Nick Knight (113 and 125* v PAK, 1996); Graeme Hick (126* v SL and 109 v AUS, 1999); Alec Stewart (101 v ZIM and 100* [carried bat] v WI, 2000); Marcus Trescothick (109 v IND and 119 v ZIM, 2002); and Andrew 'Freddie' Flintoff (106 v NZ and 123 v WI, 2004).

Pakistan – Ramiz Raja (116* and 107* v SL, 1990); Inzamam-Ul-Haq (101 and 117 v SL, 1992); Saleem Elahi (107 and 108 v ZIM, 2002); and Yousuf Youhana (129 v SRL and 125 v NZL, 2002).

West Indies – Gordon Greenidge (104 and 133* v NZ, 1987); Desmond Haynes (102* and 104* v AUS, 1984); Wavell Hinds (125* and 103* v AUS, 2003); and Chris Gayle (140 and 101 v IND, 2002).

Sri Lanka – Kumar Sangakarra (100* v PAK and 103* v KEN, 2003); and Roshan Mahanama (119* and 108 v ZIM, 1994).

South Africa: Jacques Kallis (107 v ENG and 125* v ZIM, 2003).

Most Centuries in Consecutive Tests

1. Sir Donald Bradman

It's no great surprise that a man with a Test average of 99.94 has scored more centuries in consecutive matches than any other cricketer. From January 1937 to July 1938 Australia's favourite son scored a ton in each of six Tests: 270, 212, 169, 144*, 102*, and 103. He also recorded centuries in four consecutive Tests on two occasions: March 1929 to July 1930 with 123, 131, 254, and 334 and November 1931 to January 1932 with 226, 116, 167, 299*.

2. Jacques Kallis

The big South African's fine form against the West Indies at the end of 2003 continued into 2004 and into the first Test against New Zealand, as Kallis hit three figures in five consecutive Tests. The big scores were 158, 177, 130*, 130*, and 150*.

3. Jack Fingleton

In the absence of Bradman, Australia were still far too good in

South Africa in early 1936, and Fingleton scored 122, 108 and 118 in his three innings as the tourists won each Test by more than an innings. In his next match, against England in Brisbane he scored 100 and followed that with a golden duck in the second innings to bring his run to an end.

4. Sir Everton Weekes
The only Test batsman to hit a century in five consecutive innings, Weekes dominated the England and India bowling attacks of 1948. Weekes hit 141 in the first innings at Kingston in March, his fourth Test match, but did not bat (DNB) in the second innings. In three Tests in India he scored 128 & DNB, 194 & DNB and 162 and 101. Then, in Madras, in his next innings he was run out for 90.

5. Neil Harvey
Another of Australia's talented post-war batsmen, Harvey's first tour of South Africa was a great success as he hit tons in all but the first Test to end the series with a Test average of 132. From the second to fifth Test he scored 178 and 23*, 2 and 151*, 56* and 100, and 116 and DNB. Harvey enjoyed the hospitality so much he later married a South African girl.

6. Sir Clyde Walcott
Immortalised as one of the 'Three W's' (Walcott, Weekes, and Worrell), Sir Clyde was an integral part of the West Indies Test side for a decade. The Bajan legend hit five centuries in four matches against England and Australia from 1954 to 55 in the Caribbean. His scores were 124 and 51*, 50 and 116, 108 and 39, and 126 and 110.

SHARP SHOOTERS

7. Ken Barrington
Starting his Test career with a duck, 34 and 18, Barrington was dropped from the England side for four years. When he returned to the international arena, he was one of the most difficult men to get out, as shown by the fact that on two occasions he reached three figures in four consecutive Tests. In the winter of 1961, he hit 139, 151*, 172, and 113* on tour in Pakistan and India. And in the summer and winter of 1967–68 he scored 148, 109*, 142, and 143.

8. Sunil Gavaskar
In 1977 'Sunny' scored 108 and 42 in the fifth Test against England in Bombay. He followed this up with a remarkable set of scores in his first three Tests in Australia, 3 and 113, 4 and 127 and 0 and 118 to become the first India international to score centuries in four back-to-back Tests.

9. Matthew Hayden
In a back-to-back, three-match series against South Africa, in the winter of 2001–02, the big Australian hit three figures in each of the home Tests: 131, 138, 105. Then, in Johannesburg he became the first of his countrymen for over 50 years to score centuries in four consecutive Tests, with his 122.

10. Rahul Dravid
In a golden spell towards the end of 2002, Dravid became the first Indian, and only the fourth man, behind Weekes, Fingleton, and Alan Melville (all of South Africa) to score a ton in four consecutive innings. After scoring 13 in the first innings, Dravid got 115 to save the second Test at Trent Bridge, 148 to help win at

Headingley, 217 to avoid defeat at a rain-affected Oval and a valiant 100 against the Windies in Bombay, before he retired hurt.

* = Not Out

Test Ducks

1. Courtney Walsh (43)

The former West Indies bowler may be one of only three cricketers to have taken over 500 Test wickets, but he also holds the unenviable crown of most Test ducks on 43. Walsh reached his lowest ebb as a batsman when he made three consecutive ducks in the 2000 Test series against Australia.

2. Shane Warne (30)

Second in the most career Test wickets table, and also second in the most career scoring ducks table, with 30. Despite holding a high score of 99 and a modest lower-order batsman average of 15.97, Warne scored three Test ducks in a row against the West Indies in 2001.

3. Glenn McGrath (28)

McGrath has managed to achieve ducks in a quarter of the 111 Tests he has played. The Australian bowler has 28 no scores to his name, including three consecutively in the 1998–99 Ashes Test against England. His batting average of 6.35 does not make for much better viewing.

4. Curtly Ambrose (26)

His aggression with a ball between his fingers was rarely matched with a bat at his hands. Ambrose scored 26 ducks from 145 innings, including three pairs, averaging 12.41 in an otherwise glittering career.

5. Mervyn Dillon (26)

Dillon has long been labelled as the natural successor to Courtney Walsh. Whether he is likely to do that in the bowling stakes is open to scrutiny, but on the batting side it certainly looks possible that he may follow the number one quacker. The West Indies bowler has achieved four consecutive ducks on two occasions, in addition to holding the highest percentage of career ducks, with 26 from 68 innings.

6. Muttiah Muralitharan (25)

Muralitharan is the king of wicket taking and not just the opposition's. The Sri Lankan bowler may hold the record for most Test career wickets, but he is also rather good at losing his own wicket at little expense. He has been out without hitting any runs on 25 occasions, scoring an average of 12.56.

One-Day International Ducks

In One-Day cricket it is important to keep the strike rate up, so a lot of batsmen will try to run before they can walk once they get out to the middle, and a lot of talented batsmen end up slogging out...

1. Wasim Akram
The legendary Pakistan all-rounder leads the way in one statistic that he may not be so happy about, with 28 ODI ducks Akram is still the biggest quacker in the short game.

2. Sanath Jayasuriya
Announcing his arrival on the One-Day scene as a key member of Sri Lanka's World Cup winning side in 1996, Jayasuriya has proved himself one of the best ODI players with his 18 centuries and his useful bowling, but he has also been out 25 times without troubling the scorers.

3. Romesh Kaluwitharana
Another World-Cup-winning Sri Lankan, 'Kalu' was the man behind the stumps in their remarkable victory and was a very useful batsman. Unfortunately, throughout his career he was out on 0 in 24 of his 181 matches.

4. Adam Parore
Another quacking keeper, Parore filled the Black Caps' gloves with distinction for a decade, during which time he made 19 ODI ducks, to go with his sparkling 108 against South Africa.

5. Salim Malik
A gifted Pakistan batsman who will be remembered for all the wrong reasons, 'Slim' was the first player to be banned for match fixing, he was also dismissed without troubling the scorers on 19 occasions in ODIs.

SHARP SHOOTERS

6. Javagal Srinath
One of India's fastest ever bowlers, Srinath didn't add much to his country's cause with the bat. His 19 ducks were allied with a spectacularly unimpressive average of 10.64.

7. Grant Flower
The younger brother of Andy Flower, Grant is a useful all-rounder for Zimbabwe with more than one hundred wickets, and 6,500 runs in ODIs, he also notched up 18 ducks.

8. Inzamam-Ul-Haq
The BIG batsman of the Pakistan side for more than a decade, he is the only man in the top ten with more than 10,000 ODI runs, although Jayasuriya's not far behind, he has 18 ducks in the short form of the game including one in the 2003 World Cup against the Netherlands.

9. Arjuna Ranatunga
Not the quickest man between the wickets, the Sri Lankan skipper still managed to keep the scoreboard ticking over once he got in, but in 18 matches he didn't even 'get in' enough to trouble the scoreboard.

10. Chaminda Vaas
He may have recorded 18 ducks in ODIs but the Sri Lankan seamer has still written his way into Aussie slang: 'Nice Chaminda' they say to a Sheila with a firm behind.

In the 90s

When batsmen approach three figures, the fielding side will always be keen to slow down the scoring rate in a bid to keep the man at the crease in the nervous nineties as long as possible. Some cricketers find the nerves get the better of them before the century mark, others are just beaten by a good ball. Here we look at the men most often out in the nineties:

1. Michael Slater, Australia (9)
The talented opener announced his arrival on the world scene as part of the victorious 1993 Ashes squad, scoring a sparkling hundred at Lord's. But his place in the record books is assured by his nine dismissals at less than ten runs short of a ton. His first, a 99 seeking his first century, was followed by 14 hundreds and 8 more nineties for Australia.

2. Steve Waugh, Australia (8)
Throughout his long career, which included a world record 168 Tests, 'Tugga' Waugh found himself dismissed in the nineties eight times. He was left hanging on 94 and 99 not out in a couple of other innings, and was once trapped leg before on 199, just one run short of his all time high score.

3. Alvin Kallicharran, West Indies (7)
One of the West Indies' most naturally gifted batsmen, Kallicharan showed no nerves on his international debut as he scored 100 not out, and followed that up with 101 in his next innings. But the nineties got their revenge on the left-hander, and he fell short of

three figures on seven occasions, and was left stranded on 92 not out once against Pakistan.

4. Rahul Dravid, India (6)

The India vice-captain got his Test career off to a great start against England at Lord's but ended up five runs short of a century at the home of cricket on his Test debut, as Chris Lewis had him caught behind on 95. Dravid has since been out on 92, 92, 93, 190, 91 and 92 which he followed with a 91 not out in his next match.

5. Brian Lara, West Indies (6)

The finest accumulator of giant scores in the modern game, with five double-hundreds, one triple century and the only 400 in Test cricket among his 26 three figures scores. The Prince of the Caribbean has been stopped in the nineties six times, and in the one-nineties once so far in his glittering Test career.

6. Rohan Kanhai, West Indies (6)

A versatile cricketer, Kanhai deputised behind the stumps on a number of occasions, and he captained the WI tour party of 1973 to a 2–0 win over England. The West Indian number three batsman hit 15 centuries, but was out in the nineties six times, including run outs on 90 and 99.

7. Gordon Greenidge, West Indies (6)

Half of the most destructive opening partnership of all time, along with Desmond Haynes, Greenidge succumbed to the nervous nineties in six of his innings, and was run out for 93 on his Test debut. He made amends with 107 in his second innings, but was subsequently out in the nineties in both innings of a Test match twice, and was once caught on 194.

8. Inzamam-ul-Haq, Pakistan (5)

Most batsmen like to keep the scoreboard ticking over, especially approaching the century mark, but quick singles have never been part of the big man's armoury. Inzi has been dismissed on scores of 95, 95, 96, 97 and 99 and was once left on 92 not out where, surprisingly, he didn't run out any of his seven partners.

9. Geoffrey Boycott, England (5)

In 108 Tests, the resolute Yorkshireman was stopped in the nineties five times. The 1973–74 season was responsible for most of these failures, as in the space of nine months the England opener got to 90 five times and only made one ton. Boycott faced more than half the balls in the innings as he was stranded on 99 against Australia at the WACA, in 1979.

10. Clem Hill, Australia (5)

Hill was the highest run scorer when Australia retained the Ashes in 1901–02 with 521 runs, at an average of 52.10, including 99, 98, and 97 in successive innings. The left-hander also scored 98 and 96 against the English and 91 not out and 191 playing South Africa.

The other Test batsmen to be dismissed five times in the nineties, are: Ken Barrington of England; Sachin Tendulkar, and Sunil Gavaskar, of India.

BOWLED OVER

Wickets from Wicketless Batsmen – Famous batsmen taking wickets in a rare bout of bowling

When a side have been in the field for a long time, the skipper will sometimes throw the ball to an unusual recipient in search of an elusive wicket. On the rare occasion that one of the 'net bowlers' comes up trumps, it looks like a masterstroke, but it is rarely repeated. Here are our top ten.

1. Michael Atherton (England)
'Athers' came on to bowl in the afternoon of the final day of the second Test against Pakistan in 1996 to give his bowlers a rest and to speed up England's slow over rate. Atherton quickly claimed the wicket of his friend and Lancashire teammate Wasim Akram who played no stroke to a leg-break and was given out leg before wicket. On discussing his second and final Test wicket, Atherton grinned and said, 'I think he misread it as a googly.'

BOWLED OVER

2. Mike Gatting (England)

The England opener picked up four wickets in his 79 Tests at an average of 79.25. As well as scoring 4,409 runs for England, 'Fat Gatt' picked up the wicket of Martin Crowe twice, as the New Zealand legend was beaten by the former Test captain's slower balls in 1984 and again in 1988 – both times in Wellington.

3. Hanif Mohammad (Pakistan)

The former Pakistan captain picked up just one wicket in his 55 Tests, when he clean bowled Pananmal Punjabi on the final day of the fourth Test against India in 1955. Mohammad finished his Test career with 3,915 runs, and a high score of 337, but a bowling strike rate of 206 balls per wicket.

4. Mark Taylor (Australia)

In a ten-year Test career Taylor distinguished himself as a very good batsman and a great captain, but as a bowler he was definitely not Test match standard. He still managed to claim one wicket, however, as Michael Bevan held Rashid Latif in the second innings of the second Test in Rawalpindi in October 1994, when the Australians used ten different bowlers.

5. Sunil Gavaskar (India)

The Indian legend played 125 Tests over sixteen years and broke many batting records, but he only ever picked up one wicket. On the final day of the first Test in Faisalabad in 1978, Gavaskar's medium paced bowling brought the wicket of legendary Pakistan batsman Zaheer Abbas, who was caught by Chetan Chauhan on 96.

6. David Gower (England)

Another great batsman with a solitary Test wicket is England's David Gower. Kapil Dev's 116 came to an end when Dilley held the catch from the bowling of Gower in the sixth Test in Kanpur on the 1981–2 tour.

7. Sir Donald Bradman (Australia)

Without question *the* finest batsman of all-time, no one ever has or ever will come close to his remarkable Test batting average of 99.94. The Don also turned his arm over occasionally, and claimed two wickets in his 52 Tests. In his early years, he trapped Ivan Barrow lbw, and just over two years later he clean bowled Wally Hammond, both at his second home, the Adelaide Oval.

8. Desmond Haynes (West Indies)

A fit and vibrant character, Haynes played 116 Tests for the West Indies, and bowled three overs in his time, as he found himself the eighth-choice bowler in three separate second innings over the course of 1980–81. In the second of these, in Lahore, Haynes got the wicket of Pakistan tail-ender Sarfraz Nawaz, who was caught by Joel Garner.

9. Sir Jack Hobbs (England)

Hobbs still rates as one of the best England batsmen of all-time, and he was also thought to be useful with the ball in hand. Despite opening the bowling in a number of matches, his only wicket in 61 Tests was that of English-born Reggie Schwarz, caught by Morice Bird at Cape Town in 1910.

10. Gary Kirsten (South Africa)

One of South Africa's finest batsmen, Kirsten made the opening spot his own for over a decade. In his early Tests he even got some reward for his right-arm off-spin, most notably bowling Mark Taylor in Adelaide in 1994. Later in the year, he claimed his only other Test wicket, that of Kiwi spinner Matthew Hart caught behind, to finish the innings with impressive figures of 1 for 0 from his two overs.

Most Test Wickets

In a Game

1. Jim Laker (19)

No other bowler has taken more than seventeen wickets in a first-class match, let alone in a Test match. The England fast bowler laid low Australia with unparalled figures of 19 for 90 – 9 for 37 in the first innings and 10 for 53 in the second – sealing an emphatic innings and a 170-run win for England, in 1956.

2. Sydney Barnes (17)

Before Laker set his unprecedented record, Barnes held the top score for wickets in a Test match, which stood for 42 years. In the second Test of England's 1914 tour of South Africa, which England won by an innings and 12 runs, Barnes picked up 17 wickets for 159, and accumulated a resounding 49 wickets over the entire series.

3. Narendra Hirwani (16)

Hirwani exploded onto the international Test scene, when at only nineteen he made it into the record books with a stunning 16 wickets for 136 runs in India's 255-run win against West Indies – record figures by a bowler on a Test debut. However, he failed to reproduce the same fun in subsequent Tests and eventually lost his place to Anil Kumble.

4. Robert Massie (16)

Australian Massie's international Test career followed a similar path to that of Hirwani. Massie's figures of 16 for 137, which helped demolish England at Lord's in 1972, were the best by a Test debutant until Hirwani bettered it sixteen years later. And like the India man, his international Test star also dwindled shortly after, as he played only five more matches before losing his place.

5. Muttiah Muralitharan (16)

The spin wizard put a spell on England's batsmen in the 1998 one-off Test match. Muralitharan took 16 for 220, to inspire Sri Lanka to their first triumph on English soil. In the second innings, 'Murali' racked up 9 wickets for a mere 65 runs, and might have claimed all ten had Alec Stewart not been run-out.

6. Joseph Briggs (15)

Nottinghamshire-born Briggs only played first-class cricket for three years, starting at the ripe old age of 38. Yet, in that period he still managed to claim one of the biggest Test match wicket hauls of all time, picking up 15 South African wickets whilst conceding a meagre 28 runs in 33.3 overs as England were victorious in the 1888 second Test by an innings and 202 runs.

7. George Lohmann (15)

Wisden's Cricketer of the Year back in 1889, Lohmann helped England to a series whitewash over South Africa between 1895 and 1896, collecting 35 wickets in the three-Test series. However, the highlight of the series for Lohmann came when he racked up fifteen dismissals in only 25.3 overs, forfeiting just 45 runs.

8. Colin Blythe (15)

Despite suffering from epilepsy, Blythe claimed more than 13 wickets in 15 separate Test matches, although most of these were in county cricket. His most significant international haul was against South Africa in 1907 taking 15 wickets for 99 runs. England won the second Test by 53 runs.

9. Hedley Verity (15)

Verity remains the only cricketer to have taken 14 wickets in one day in a Test match. This happened in the England v. Australia second Test at Lord's in 1934. During the Test he took a total of fifteen Australian scalps for 104 runs, as England won at a canter by an innings and 38 runs.

10. Sir Richard Hadlee (15)

Hadlee played a huge part in New Zealand's first Test win in Australia, between 1985 and 1986. He produced his greatest bowling performance with 9–52 in the first innings and captured a total of 15 wickets in the match, as well as scoring 54 with the bat.

11. Wilfred Rhodes (15)

Rhodes shares the honour of taking most wickets in an England v. Australia match with his eventual successor in the England set-up,

Hedley Verity. Rhodes collected his record, of 15 wickets, in Melbourne, Australia in the 1903–04 second Test, which England won by 185 runs.

12. Harbhajan Singh (15)

Australia were once again the victim of a one-man, huge wicket haul, when Singh collected 15 Aussie wickets for 217 runs, as India won by two wickets, to clinch a 2–1 series win and lift the 2001 Border Gavaskar Trophy.

In a Season

1. Dennis Lillee

Lillee's remarkable 85-wicket haul in thirteen Tests in 1981 is still unbeaten, and it was achieved with 21 Indian wickets in three tests at the start of the year, overtaking Richie Benaud's record of 248 Test wickets for Australia before claiming 39 wickets in six Tests in England, including 11 for 159 at The Oval. Returning to Australia, Lillee continued his fine form against Pakistan, and took career best figures of 7 for 83 against the West Indies in the first innings at the MCG.

2. Allan Donald

The first South African bowler to reach 300 Test wickets, Donald enjoyed his most prolific form in 1998. Recording 80 wickets in fourteen Tests, including 33 in five Tests in England and three wickets in Australia, with the rest of his mighty haul coming on home turf against Sri Lanka, Pakistan, and the West Indies.

3. Muttiah Muralitharan

Sri Lanka's finest ever bowler, 'Murali' bettered his fine 2000 total in the following year with 80 wickets in just 12 Tests in 2001. The year got off to a relatively slow start with one South African wicket in the defeat at Newlands, and fourteen as England recorded a three-match series win in Sri Lanka. But with India, Bangladesh, the West Indies, and Zimbabwe as the tourists, the spinner claimed 65 wickets in eight Tests, with four successive 10-wicket matches.

4. Joel Garner

'Big Bird' was a key part of one of the most devastating pace attacks of all-time, and such was the talent through the side that the workload was shared to such an extent that Garner only recorded a five-wicket innings on seven occasions, four of which were in 1984 as he claimed 79 wickets in fifteen Tests against Australia, in the Caribbean and on tour, and in England.

5. Kapil Dev

Kapil Dev was India's finest pace bowler, and one of the best all-rounders to grace the game. His bowling was at its most effective in 1983, when he claimed 75 wickets in eighteen Tests, the highlight of which was his 9 for 83 against the West Indies, in the third Test in Ahmedabad, which wasn't enough to prevent the tourists winning.

6. Muttiah Muralitharan

'Murali' had an incredible year in 2000 with 75 wickets in just ten Tests. Including 13 for 171 against South Africa at Galle and 11 for 161 against the same opponents in Kingsmead. As well as home and away series against the Proteas, Sri Lanka also played back-to-back series against Pakistan.

7. Kapil Dev
Kapil Dev made his Test debut against Pakistan in October 1978, and by the end of 1979 he had set a new record for wickets in a calendar year as he claimed 74 victims in seventeen Tests. He started the year with eleven West Indian wickets in three Tests in India, before getting sixteen wickets in his first tour of England, and 28 and 19 as Australia and then Pakistan toured the subcontinent.

8. Malcolm Marshall
Marshall took some time to break up the legendary attack of Roberts, Holding, Croft, and Garner, but by 1984 he was considered the finest fast bowler in the world, and he took 73 wickets in thirteen Tests. A true testament to his courage and resilience came at Headingley, when he broke his left thumb in the field on the first day, batted one-handed long enough to guide Larry Gomes to a century and claimed 7 for 53 in the second innings against England.

9. Shane Warne
Australia's finest spin bowler got off to a slow start in 1993, taking 1 for 16 in his sixth Test, against West Indies at the SCG, and claiming just one more wicket in the next two Tests. After taking seventeen wickets in three Tests in New Zealand, Warne took 34 wickets in six Tests in England, including the 'ball of the century' to dismiss Mike Gatting, before returning home to take his total 72 wickets in sixteen Tests for the year with the visit of New Zealand and South Africa.

10. Graham McKenzie

In 1964 'Garth' broke Sydney Barnes' record of 61 wickets in a calendar year, a total that had stood untouched since 1912. The Western Australian fast bowler set a new total of 71 wickets in fourteen Tests, which lasted for another fifteen years, including 29 wickets in five Tests in England.

In a Career

1. Shane Warne (537)

Despite missing a year following a failed drugs test, the ebullient Australian has fought back to reclaim his place as cricket's greatest Test wicket-taker. Warne's unerring accuracy at turning the ball huge distances has re-defined the art of leg spin bowling, and paid dividends with 537 wickets in 115 tests, making an average of 25.59.

2. Muttiah Muralitharan (532)

Hot on the heels of Warne in the Test wicket stakes, 'Murali' has also been beset with controversy, though his troubles stem from a bent arm bowling action, after being called for throwing in the 1995–96 and 1998–99 tours of Australia. The spin bowler became the first Sri Lankan to reach 100 test wickets and he currently stands at 532 wickets, averaging 22.78.

3. Courtney Walsh (519)

While Warne and Muralitharan continue to battle it out for the Test wicket top spot, West Indies' Walsh can lay claim to being unchallenged as top Test wicket-taker for more than four years, between 2000 and 2004, when he overtook Kapil Dev, and finished his career with 519 dismissals at an average rate of 24.44, from 132 tests.

4. Glenn McGrath (446)
One of world cricket's most devastating fast bowlers, McGrath remains at the forefront of Australia's fierce bowling attack, despite being plagued with injuries, with impressive figures of 446 removals in a century of Tests, at 21.74.

5. Kapil Dev (434)
One of the best all-rounders of all time, he led India to their only World Cup triumph in 1983. Voted India Cricketer of the Century during 2002, he played 131 Tests and skittled 434 opponents at a rate of 29.65, in a distinguished sixteen-year international career.

6. Sir Richard Hadlee (431)
Another fine all-rounder, Hadlee was a right-arm pace bowler who was knighted for services to cricket before his playing career ended in 1990. Universally regarded as New Zealand's greatest, he collected 431 wickets in just 86 tests, at 22.30.

7. Anil Kumble (417)
Having taken 417 wickets in 87 tests, averaging 28.06, Kumble remains a lethal weapon in India's arsenal. On 7 February 1999 the leg-spinner achieved a feat managed just once previously in Test cricket, when he claimed all ten wickets in a Test innings, in the second Test second innings of India's 212-run win over bitter rivals Pakistan.

8. Wasim Akram (414)

Rated by many as the best left-arm fast bowler of all-time, and his record certainly appears to back this up. In 104 tests, at 23.62, 414 batsmen fell victim to the Pakistani's high-speed, deceptive, ball-concealing action, which can deliver yorkers as effectively as it can bouncers.

9. Curtly Ambrose (405)

Standing at the colossal height of 6' 7", Ambrose was always a fearsome sight for any batsman. Among the West Indian's 405 Test wickets, his finest moment arguably came in 1993–94, taking 6 for 24, which helped hustle England all out for 46. He retired in 2000 averaging 20.99 in 98 Tests.

10. Ian Botham (383)

'Beefy' is regarded as one of cricket's most colourful characters, equally at home making headlines during play as he was away from cricket. Off the pitch, Botham was suspended in 1989 for smoking cannabis, while on it the all-rounder smoked 383 Test victims at 28.40, from 102 Tests.

Most One-Day Wickets

In One-Day international cricket the bowlers are limited, typically, to ten overs, which makes it all the more remarkable when they can claim more than half the available wickets in the innings. Here we look at some of the players who have dominated One-Day international matches with the ball in hand.

In a Game

1. Chaminda Vaas
The Sri Lankan pace man is the only man to capture an ODI eight-wicket haul. In Colombo, in December 2001, Vaas claimed the first eight Zimbabwean wickets for the loss of only nineteen runs, including a hat-trick of Stuart Carlisle, Craig Wishart, and Tatenda Taibu. With the shine disappearing off the ball, Murali came on to finish the job, with the last two wickets as the visitors were all out for 38.

2. Glenn McGrath
Having set Namibia 302 to win in Pool A of the Preliminary round at the 2003 Cricket World Cup, Australia were typically merciless against the minnows. McGrath was at the forefront of the bowling attack, finishing with figures of 7 for 15, as the Africans were all out for a paltry 45 in Potchefstroom.

3. Andy Bichel
Australia's perennial twelfth man put in a match-winning performance against England in the 2003 Cricket World Cup. Only playing because of a heel injury suffered by Jason Gillespie, Bichel claimed 7 for 20 with a breathtaking display of bowling, before sharing a 73-run ninth-wicket partnership with Michael Bevan to guide Australia to victory with just two balls to spare.

4. Muttiah Muralitharan
Sri Lanka's finest bowler sits behind Chaminda Vaas in this list, but few others. Murali's 7 for 30 in the Champions Trophy may not match his fellow countryman's best haul, but the spinner took the

wicket of Sachin Tendulkar and six of his team-mates as India were all out for 226 in Sharjah, back in 2000.

5. Waqar Younis

One of the finest exponents of reverse swing in cricket, Younis captained his side to a fine victory over England on the back of figures of seven for 36. The skipper claimed the first seven wickets of the English innings, and when a pitch invasion halted the game with Pakistan four runs from victory, England became the first ever side to concede an international match.

6. Aaqib Javed

Javed spent much of his career in the shadows of Waqar Younis and Wasim Akram, but he was very much centre stage as Pakistan overcame India in the final of the 1991 Wills Trophy in Sharjah. Javed recorded figures of 7 for 37, including a memorable hat-trick of Ravi Shastri, Mohammad Azharuddin, and Sachin Tendulkar.

7. Winston Davis

Davis came on at first change to relieve Michael Holding and Anderson Roberts, and went on to claim 7 for 51 against Australia in the 1983 World Cup at Headingley. These figures remain the best figures for a West Indian bowler in One-Day cricket, from this 60-over match.

8. Anil Kumble

India's best spinner has sometimes struggled outside of his homeland, but on the sub-continent he is majestic. Kumble produced his most impressive ODI figures in 1993 at Eden Gardens, Kolkata, as he took 6 for 12 tearing through the West Indies middle order and tail in just six overs and one ball.

9. Gary Gilmour
He only played five ODIs, but held the best Australian One-Day figures for 28 years. In the semi-final of the 1975 World Cup at Headingley, a 60-over match, Gilmour turned in a Man-of-the-Match performance with 6 for 14 with the ball in hand, and 28 runs from 28 balls faced, to set up a final clash with West Indies at Lord's, where his figures of 5 for 48 couldn't prevent defeat.

10. Imran Khan
Arguably cricket's greatest all-rounder and undisputably Pakistan's best, Khan put in a fantastic performance with the ball against India at Sharjah in 1985, getting figures of 6 for 14 as their great rivals were skittled out for 125. Unfortunately, the political hopeful failed to reproduce the heroics with the bat, getting a duck as they collapsed to 87 all out.

Other bowlers to claim 'six-for' in an ODI: Waqar Younis (four times), Henry Olonga (twice), Colin Croft, Shoaib Akhtar, Azhar Mahmood, Brian Strang, Fidel Edwards, Ashish Nehra, Shane Bond, Allan Donald, Scott Styris, Chaminda Vaas, Balfour Patterson, Sanath Jayasuriya, Shaun Pollock, Abdul Razzaq, Kenneth MacLeay, Sir Viv Richards, Ajit Agarkar, Lance Klusener, and Anthony Gray.

BOWLED OVER

In a Season

1. Saqlain Mushtaq
One of the all-time top ten wicket takers in One-Day cricket, Mushtaq's off breaks have beaten a great number of batsmen throughout his career. In 1997, he was at his best mixing up all his different deliveries often to the same result, as he claimed 69 wickets in 36 matches, at an average of just 18.74.

2. Saqlain Mushtaq
Before breaking his own record Saqi destroyed Shane Warne's 1994 tally of 50 by claiming 64 wickets in 1996. In 33 matches over the course of the year the Pakistan offspinner consistently picked up key scalps before claiming two five-fors in December against New Zealand and Australia.

3. Shane Warne
In a World Cup year Warne produced his best One-Day form. He thrives on pressure and delivered Man-of-the-Match performances in the semi-final and final, with figures of 4 for 29 and 4 for 33 respectively. In 1999, he got 62 wickets in total from 37 ODIs.

4. Abdul Razzaq
A potential successor to Imran Khan's all-rounder spot in the Pakistan side, Razzaq's bowling was at its best in the One-Day game in 2000, as he claimed 61 wickets in 38 matches, at an average of 22.46. His best figures came at the Bellerive Oval, where he took five for 48 to defeat India.

5. Anil Kumble
India's leading One-Day wicket-taker, Kumble was at his most prolific in 1996, taking 61 wickets in 32 matches. His best performance of the year came against their fiercest rivals, as he took four Pakistan wickets for just 12 runs in Toronto.

6. Shaun Pollock
South Africa's leading wicket-taker in both forms of the game, the former skipper comes from fine cricket stock with both his father and his uncle excelling at international level. The younger Pollock claimed 61 victims in 28 ODIs in 2000.

7. Waqar Younis
One of the leading One-Day wicket-takers of all time, the former Pakistan captain was at his most successful in 1996, when he took 60 scalps in 35 matches. Waqar's best figures came in November against New Zealand, where he claimed six Black Cap wickets for the loss of 44 runs in Sharjah.

8. Ajit Agarkar
In his debut year in One-Day international cricket, India's potential successor to Kapil Dev, became the fastest man to 50 ODI wickets. Agarkar brought up his half century in just 23 matches, going on to finish 1998 with a total of 58 from 30 games.

9. Muttiah Muralitharan
No bowling list would be complete without an entry from Murali. Sri Lanka's finest picked up 56 wickets in 2001 from 33 matches. The spin bowler was also extremely economical with the wickets

coming at an average of 18.20 runs, and just 3.30 runs per over during the year.

10. Shaun Pollock
Following his fine form of 2000, Pollock struggled the next year, claiming just 27 wickets, but in 2002 the South African captain was back leading by example, with 54 wickets coming from his 33 matches.

In a Career

1. Wasim Akram (502)
The only bowler ever to take over 500 wickets in One-Day international cricket, during 356 games for Pakistan. The left-arm fast bowler, probably the foremost exponent of reverse swing, claimed 502 wickets at an average of 23.53 in a nineteen-year career, the highlight of which was winning the 1992 World Cup with Pakistan.

2. Waqar Younis (416)
Another member of Pakistan's triumphant World Cup team of 1992. Nicknamed the 'Burewala Express', after his home town, Younis was the fastest player ever to reach 200 One-Day wickets. He captained Pakistan in the 2003 World Cup before bowing out with figures of 416 wickets at an average of 23.84.

3. Muttiah Muralitharan (366)
In 237 ODIs, Muralitharan has claimed 366 scalps at a rate of 22.14. The Sri Lankan right-arm off-break bowler became only the

fourth bowler in history to claim 30 wickets in both Test and One-Day cricket when he bowled England's James Anderson in a One-Dayer in January 2003.

4. Anil Kumble (321)

One of the finest spin bowlers of the last twenty years, Kumble is a master of disguising the flight of the ball, mixing up the deliveries of his ball on a constant basis. He has been repaid with 321 One-Day dismissals, averaging 30.70, and impressive best figures of 6 for 12 coming against West Indies in 1993.

5. Chaminda Vaas (321)

Possesses one of the longest names in cricket in Warnakulasuriya Patabendige Ushantha Joseph Chaminda Vaas. The Sri Lankan seamer boasts the best ever bowling figures in an ODI, when he achieved 8 for 19 against Zimbabwe in 2001. Yet the records do not end there. The 1996 World Cup winner also holds the distinction of being the only man to take a hat-trick with the first three deliveries of a Test or One-Day game, when in a 2003 World Cup Pool B match against Bangladesh he finished the first over on 4 wickets for 5 runs. It is only the third hat-trick in World Cup history, and his record currently stands at 321 wickets conceding an average of 26.10.

6. Javagal Srinath (315)

Only Dennis Lillee and Waqar Younis have taken 100 wickets in fewer limited overs matches. The paceman played in three World Cups for India, before retiring after the 2003 tournament with 315 removals at a rate of 28.09 to his name, since making his debut against Pakistan in 1991.

7. Shaun Pollock (305)

The South Africa captain averages 23.70 with the ball and has taken fifteen four-wicket hauls in his One-Day international career to date, his best being 6 for 35 against the West Indies in 1998. He is the son of former South African fast bowler Peter Pollock, and has so far clocked up 305 wickets.

8. Shane Warne (291)

Known more for his Test rather than One-Day exploits, Warne was instrumental in Australia's charge to World Cup glory in 1999, claiming 4 for 29 in a ten-over spell in the semi-final against South Africa and being named Man of the Match in the final, after another four-wicket haul against Pakistan. He has accumulated 291 wickets in his ODI career at an average of 25.82.

9. Glenn McGrath (289)

The 2003 World Cup saw McGrath produce his finest One-Day performance, skittling seven batsman at the expense of only fifteen runs, with Namibia the victims in a 256-run mauling. In total, McGrath has 289 wickets to his name, at an average 22.67, and is well on course to beat Wasim Akram's record of 236 maidens, trailing the retired Pakistan bowler by thirteen.

10. Saqlain Mushtaq (288)

Despite making his ODI debut against Sri Lanka in 1995, it was not until 1996–97 that Mushtaq came to the forefront of One-Day cricket when he produced five-wicket hauls over Australia and New Zealand. The Pakistan spin wizard is the fastest bowler to reach 100 One-Day wickets and also belongs to an élite group of bowlers who have twice claimed hat-tricks in One-Day cricket.

His record currently stands at 288 wickets from 169 ODIs, averaging a thrifty 21.79.

Hat-tricks

Footballers get to keep the ball when they score a hat-trick – three goals in a game. But a bowler has the far harder task of taking three wickets with successive balls to claim a hat-trick in cricket – and they don't even get to keep the ball! Here is a rundown of the hat-trick heroes around the cricketing globe.

Australia

The first bowler to perform a hat-trick was Australia's **Fredrick 'Demon' Spofforth**. The Demon was playing for Australia against England, at Melbourne, on 2 January 1879 in only the third Test match ever contested. He dismissed Vernon Royle, Francis MacKinnon and Thomas Emmett from three successive balls. That reduced England to 26 for 7 in the first innings. Thanks to Spofforth's final tally of thirteen wickets, Australia won the Test by ten wickets.

Only three bowlers – off spinner **Hugh Trumble**, leg-spinner **Thomas James Matthews** (both Australians), and speedster **Wasim Akram** of Pakistan – have the honour of recording two Test match hat-tricks.

Trumble accomplished the feat both times against England at the same Melbourne venue, but in two separate series. The first time came in January 1902, in the second Ashes Test, when he claimed the wickets of Arthur Jones, John Gunn and Sydney Barnes in England's second innings. The second success came two years later in March 1904, the fifth Ashes Test, and Trumble's farewell first-class game. This time Trumble dismissed Bernard Bosanquet, Pelham Warner and Arthur Lilley. Australia won the Test both times.

Matthews is the only bowler in cricket history to have performed the feat of a hat-trick in each innings of the same Test, both instances being on the afternoon of 28 May 1912 against South Africa, at Manchester, in a triangular tournament. He captured only six wickets in the Test and all were claimed without any assistance from the fielders. Thomas Ward, who bagged a 'King Pair' (two Golden ducks) was the third victim in both of Matthews' hat-tricks, as Australia coasted to an innings and an 88-run win.

Australia's other hat-tricksters are **Lindsay Kline** (2nd Test v South Africa, won by an innings and 141 runs, 31 December 1957), **Bruce Reid** (ODI v New Zealand, won by 99 runs, 29 January 1986), **Merv Hughes** (2nd Test v West Indies, lost by 169 runs, 2 December 1988), **Damien Fleming** (on his debut in the drawn 2nd Test v Pakistan, 5 October 1994), **Shane Warne** (2nd Test v England, won by 295 runs, 24 December 1994), **Anthony Stuart** (ODI v Pakistan, won by 3 wickets, 16 January 1997), **Glenn McGrath** (2nd Test v West Indies won by an innings and 27 runs, 1 December 2000) and **Brett Lee** (ODI v Kenya, won by five wickets, 15 March 2003).

Bangladesh

Alok Kapali became the first, and so far the only, Bangladeshi bowler to manage a hat-trick in international cricket, when he dismissed Pakistan's Shabbir Ahmed, Danish Kaneria and Umar Gal with consecutive balls at Peshawar in August 2003 in the second Test. The all-rounder was only nineteen at the time, and his performance secured his side their first first-innings lead at the 23rd attempt, though they eventually lost the Test by nine wickets.

England

Three bowlers have the proud distinction of recording a hat-trick on their Test debut. Medium pacer **Maurice Allom** is one of them. Bowling his eighth over on his first day in Test cricket on 10 January 1930 against New Zealand at Christchurch, Allom actually captured four wickets in five balls, to help England to an eight-wicket win.

England's **Willie Bates** also deserves special mention here. In the 1882–83 Melbourne Test against Australia, Bates, by dismissing Percy McDonnell, George Giffen and George Bonnor, not only registered the hat-trick – the first Englishman to do so – but also scored 55 runs, the second highest on either side in the Test and went on to claim seven wickets in each innings – 7 for 28 off 26.2 overs, followed by 7 for 74 runs – for a match haul of 14 for 102 runs. Thanks to his excellent bowling, England won the Test by an innings and 27 runs, which was the first victory by the margin of an innings in Tests.

BOWLED OVER

At the moment the latest bowler to take a hat-trick in one-day international cricket is English. On 1 September 2004, **Steve Harmison** achieved the feat by dismissing Mohammad Kaif, Lakshmipathy Balaji and Ashish Nehra to finish India's innings in the 44th over and help England to a seven-wicket win.

Other England hat-trick takers are: **Johnny Briggs** (2nd Test v Australia, lost by 72 runs, 29 January 1892), **George Lohmann** (1st Test v South Africa, England won by 288 runs, 13 February 1896), **John Hearne** (3rd Test v Australia, draw, 29 June 1899), **Thomas Goddard** (1st Test v South Africa, draw, 24 December 1938), **Peter Loader** (4th Test v West Indies, England won by an innings and 5 runs, 25 July 1957), **Dominic Cork** (4th Test v West Indies, England won by 6 wickets, 27 July 1995), **Darren Gough** (5th Test v Australia, lost by 98 runs, 2 January 1999), **James Anderson** (ODI seven-wicket win v Pakistan, 20 June 2003) and **Matthew Hoggard** (3rd Test v West Indies, England won by 8 wickets, 1 April 2004).

India

Chetan Sharma was India's first-ever hat-trick hero when, in 1987, he skittled New Zealand's Kenneth Rutherford, Ian Smith and Ewen Chatfield in consecutive deliveries to become the first man to score a hat-trick in a World Cup, and give India a nine-wicket win.

Kapil Dev then repeated the trick against Sri Lanka, at the expense of Roshan Mahanama, Rumesh Ratnayake and Sanath Jayasuriya in the 1990–91 Asia Cup which India won by seven wickets.

Harbhajan Singh then became India's first Test hat-trick man when he took the stumps of Ricky Ponting, Adam Gilchrist and Shane Warne in the 2001 second Test of a 171-run win for India.

New Zealand

The most recent hat-trick in international cricket came on 19 October 2004, when James Franklin dismissed Bangladesh's Manjural Rana and Mohammad Rafique with the last two balls of his opening over and then removed Tapash Baisya with the first delivery of his next over. New Zealand won that first Test by an innings and 99 runs.

The first-ever Kiwi hat-trick came courtesy of **Peter Petherick** on his Test debut against Pakistan in Lahore in 1976 at the ripe old age of 34, and what an illustrious triumvirate it was: Javed Miandad, Wasim Raja and Intikhab Alam. However, despite that setback, Pakistan won the first Test by six wickets.

New Zealand's solitary One-Day hat-trick came at the expense of India's Kapil Dev, Salil Ankola, Nayan Mongia, with **Daniel Morrison** the benefactor in a 28-run win on 25 March 1994.

Pakistan

Wasim Akram is Pakistan's hat-trick specialist. No other cricketer has ever taken four hat-tricks in international cricket.

His Test hat-tricks both came against Sri Lanka in the 1999 Asian Test Championship. Akram claimed the first of his hat-tricks in a draw on 4 March, the victims being Romesh Kaluwitharana, Mapa Bandaratilleke and Pramodya Wickramasinghe, and picked up his second Test hat-trick eight days later, taking the wickets of Avishka Gunawardene, Chaminda Vaas and Mahela Jayawardene, as Pakistan won by an innings and 175 runs.

Wasim's ODI hat-tricks also came in quick succession. On 14 October 1989 he achieved his first at the expense of West Indies trio Jeff Dujon, Curtly Ambrose and Malcolm Marshall, in an 11-run win for Pakistan. Less than seven months later, Akram repeated the feat, this time skittling Australia's Merv Hughes, Carl Rackemann and Terry Alderman, as Pakistan won the match by 36 runs.

Only two other bowlers have achieved two hat-tricks in ODI cricket: Sri Lanka's Chaminda Vaas and Akram's fellow countryman **Saqlain Mushtaq**. Mushtaq claimed both his ODI hat-tricks at Zimbabwe's expense. In 1996 it was Gavin Rennie, John Rennie and Andrew Whittal who fell foul of Mushtaq's bowling and, in 1999, it was Henry Olonga, Adam Huckle and Pommie Mbangwa, as Pakistan sealed victory in both ties.

Pakistan possess a third famous hat-trick specialist in **Mohammad Sami,** who, besides Akram, is the only man to have taken a hat-trick in both One-Day and Test cricket.

Amazingly, he accomplished this feat within a month. In an ODI on 15 February 2002 against West Indies, Sami took the scalps of Ridley Jacobs, Corey Collymore, and Cameron Cuffy, as Pakistan won by 51 runs. Then, in a Test match, nineteen days later, against

Sri Lanka, Sami doubled his hat-trick tally by taking the wickets of Buddika Fernando, Nuwan Zoysa and Muttiah Muralitharan. However, it was not enough to stop Sri Lanka winning the Test by eight wickets.

Pakistan's other hat-trick exploits have come courtesy of **Jalal-ud-din** (the first in ODI history, v Australia, won by 59 runs 20 September1982), **Aaqib Javed** (ODI v India, won by 72 runs 25 October 1991), **Waqar Younis** (ODI v New Zealand, won by five wickets 19 December 1994) and **Abdul Razzaq** (2nd Test v Sri Lanka, won by an innings and 163 runs 21 June 2000).

South Africa

Geoffrey Griffin is the only South African ever to have claimed a hat-trick in international cricket, however his feat is shrouded in controversy. Handicapped by an accident as a schoolboy, which left him unable to fully straighten his right arm, he was further burdened when 'throwing' became cricket's major issue. Despite murmurings about his action, he joined his country's 1960 tour of England. He was no-balled in county matches at Nottingham and Southampton, before claiming his famous hat-trick in the second Test, the first man to do so at Lord's. However, South Africa lost the Test by an innings and 73 runs, and Griffin was no-balled eleven times for throwing. To make matters worse, he was again no-balled in an exhibition match staged in the presence of the Queen, as the Test ended early, and was forced to complete his over underarm, putting a swift end to his international bowling career.

BOWLED OVER

Sri Lanka

Sri Lanka possess a hat-trick specialist in **Chaminda Vaas**, who is one of only three bowlers ever to have taken two hat-tricks in One-Day international history.

Vaas took his first hat-trick against Zimbabwe in 2001, finishing with eight for 19 – the best-ever bowling figures in an ODI. The match lasted just twenty overs as Zimbabwe were dismissed for the lowest ever One-Day score of 38, in 15.4 overs.

His second hat-trick in the Group B World Cup ten-wicket win over Bangladesh in 2003 also made history. The Sri Lankan seamer took a hat-trick with the first three balls of the match – the only man in either Test or One-Day cricket to do so, and achieved this despite suffering with a sore back.

The only feat to come close to Vaas's in top-class cricket was recorded by team-mate **Nuwan Zoysa**, when he took a hat-trick with his first three balls of the match, in the second over of the second Test against Zimbabwe, when Sri Lanka claimed a six-wicket win on 26 November 1999 in Harare.

West Indies

Jermaine Lawson became the first West Indian to achieve this rare feat on Caribbean soil, having just recovered from a bout of chickenpox, when he dismissed Brett Lee and Stuart MacGill, with the second and third balls off his 33rd over in Australia's first innings, and Justin Langer, with his first ball in the second innings of the third Test at Bridgewater on 5 May 2003, which Australia won by nine wickets. He is the fourth West Indian to have realised this accomplishment, which have all come in Test matches.

The first was **Wesley Hall** in 1959 who bowled Mushtaq Mohammad, Fazal Mahmood and Nasim-Ul-Ghani of Pakistan, in an innings and 156-run win for West Indies in the third Test at Bagh-e-Jinnah, Lahore.

Lance Gibbs, grabbed a triple in the 1961 fourth Test stalemate with Australia, and **Courtney Walsh** captured a split hat-trick in 1988 to help West Indies beat Australia by nine wickets.

Zimbabwe

There have been two hat-trick heroes for Zimbabwe over the years. **Eddo Brandes** achieved world fame in 1997 as the chicken farmer who took a hat-trick against England in the form of Nick Knight, John Crawley and Nasser Hussain's wickets, setting the seal on a 3–0, One-Day series victory.

Andy Blignaut grabbed a Test hat-trick in Harare in 2004 against Bangladesh. Hannan Sarkar, Mohammed Ashraful and Mushfiqur Rahman were the victims in a first Test, 183-run win.

My Bunny

Some bowlers just seem to own the wicket of some of the batsmen they face. When they walk out to the crease, it is often a question of when, rather than who, is going to get the man out, as old rivals go toe to toe once again. These are the only eleven bowlers who have got the same man out at least ten times.

1. Glenn McGrath (Australia) & Michael Atherton (England)

The biggest bunny of them all, 'Pigeon' was responsible for getting rid of England's long-time opener and skipper, nineteen times. Athers was invariably caught behind, either by the keeper or one of the slips.

2. Sir Alec Bedser (England) & Arthur Morris (Australia)

Bedser led the England bowling attack almost single-handedly at times, and regularly exploited Morris' fallibility against the swinging ball around the leg-stump, dismissing him eighteen times. Bedser dismissed the Aussie opener on his 29th birthday and presented him with a book called *Better Cricket*. In his next match, Morris made his highest Test score of 206, in the fourth Test at Adelaide.

3. Curtly Ambrose (West Indies) & Michael Atherton (England)

Atherton was considered the key wicket in the England side for a number of years and Ambrose was always keen to make inroads to a batting line-up. With the new ball in his hand Curtly was a menace to any batsman and he had the pleasure beating of Atherton on seventeen occasions.

4. Courtney Walsh (West Indies) & Michael Atherton (England)

What is it about Atherton? It makes one wonder why everyone didn't work him out. Walsh, the West Indies' leading Test wicket taker of all time, certainly did. Like his international bowling partner Ambrose, he was especially dangerous with the new ball, and always likely to get an innings off to a good start. Facing England, he did that regularly, dismissing Athers seventeen times.

5. Malcolm Marshall (West Indies) & Graham Gooch (England)
Before Ambrose/Walsh and Atherton came along, there was another West Indies bowler who seemingly had an England opener in his pocket. Marshall would work meticulously on a batsman's weak points until he got the better of them, as he did with Gooch in sixteen innings.

6. Curtly Ambrose (West Indies) & Mark Waugh (Australia)
The giant West Indies bowler didn't just save all his best efforts for Atherton and other openers, he also relished the Australian middle order, and Mark Waugh in particular, as the talented batsman fell to Ambrose fifteen times.

7. Hugh Trumble (Australia) & Tom Hayward (England)
An historic pair, England opener Hayward was the first man to score 100 first-class centuries, and Australian off-spinner Trumble was the first man to claim two Test hat-tricks. Of his 141 wickets, fifteen of them were Hayward's.

8. Courtney Walsh (West Indies) & Ian Healy (Australia)
The most successful wicket-keeper of them all, Healy was the heartbeat of the Australia side for a decade, and saved his best for the Ashes, where he was regularly a thorn in the England side with his glove work and his batting. Against the West Indies, Healy wasn't as fruitful, and was beaten by Walsh on fifteen occasions.

9. Geoff Lawson (Australia) & David Gower (England)
A hostile quick bowler, Lawson took the mantle of Australia's most dangerous pace man from Dennis Lillee. The New South Wales player managed to use his pace to good effect in claiming 180 Test wickets, fourteen of which had the curly-haired Gower's name on them.

10. Monty Noble (Australia) & Dick Lilley (England)
Arguably Australia's greatest all-round cricketer, Noble excelled as a batsman, bowler, fieldsman and captain. He also has the highest percentage (11.57) of one man's wickets making up his total – of Noble's 121 total, England keeper Lilley's name appears fourteen times.

11. Shane Warne (Australia A) & Alec Stewart (England)
In an English record 133 Test appearances, England's batting, keeping, all-rounder one-time captain batted from one to seven, but no matter where he appeared on the order against Australia, there was always a good chance it was Warnie who would get him in the end, as he did in fourteen innings.

Fastest Bowlers

1. Shoaib Akhtar   161.3 kph/100.04 mph
2. Brett Lee   160.7 kph/99.8 mph
3. Jeff Thompson   160.7 kph/99.8 mph
4. Andy Roberts   157.4 kph/97.8 mph
5. Nantie Hayward   154.5 kph/96.0 mph
6. Shane Bond   153.4 kph/95.3 mph

7. Jermaine Lawson 153.2 kph/95.2 mph
8. Waqar Younis   153.0 kph/95.1 mph
9. Steve Harmison 151.9 kph/94.5 mph
10. Ashish Nehra   149.7 kph/93.0 mph

1. Shoaib Akhtar
Pakistan's current paceman holds the record for the fastest delivery – recorded at 161.3 Kph/100.04 mph against New Zealand in 2002. The 'Rawalpindi Express' was the first person to break the 100 mph barrier when bowling to England's Nick Knight and the nuggety left-hander was so stunned by the pace he tucked it to mid-wicket for a dot ball.

2. Brett Lee
The blonde quickie has threatened to usurp Akhtar's record-breaking title by recording an impressive 160.7 kph/99.8 mph delivery speed. Pakistan's Abdul Razzaq can testify to the power of Lee's deliveries, suffering a broken wrist at the hands of the Australian.

3. Jeff Thompson
The Sydney-born surfer held the record in the 1970s, recording a speed of 160.7 kph/99.8 mph in 1975 in Perth. However, the accuracy of the freeze frame photography used to calculate the speed has been called into question.

4. Andy Roberts
Winning the Wisden Cricketer of the Year in 1975, Roberts was the quickest man to take 100 wickets for the West Indies in his day, taking just two and a half years. His fastest recorded delivery of 157.4 kph/97.8 mph makes him a force to be reckoned with.

5. Nantie Hayward

The South African starlet, has been hailed as the new Allan Donald. Recording a delivery speed of 154.5 kph/96.0 mph, his early days playing provincial baseball have no doubt contributed to the development of his efficient bowling action.

6. Shane Bond

The New Zealand and Warwickshire bowler has recorded an impressive delivery speed of 153.4 kph/95.3 mph. A former policeman, Bond has been plagued by a serious back injury in recent years and may never reach the same top speeds again.

7. Jermaine Lawson

Despite recording an official speed of 153.2 kph/95.2 mph, Lawson has suffered fierce criticism in recent years. The legitimacy of his untidy bowling action has been questioned by many and resulted in an investigation by the ICC in 2003, by which he was eventually cleared.

8. Waqar Younis

The former Pakistan captain has recorded his fastest delivery at 153.0 kph/95.1 mph. Retiring in April 2004, Younis was renowned for a lethal late in swinging yorker. He is no stranger to the record books either, as the youngest player to take 200 Test wickets and the fastest player to take 200 One-Day wickets.

9. Steve Harmison

England's quickest Test match bowler ever regularly hits the mid nineties without too much fuss, but it is his new found control that makes him one of the toughest propositions in world cricket. Plus with his towering height he can extract the steepling bounce to cause real problems – the 'baby Ambrose' nickname he was given in the Windies is more than appropriate.

10. Ashish Nehra

India's injury-prone bowler has demonstrated his power and efficiency by recording a delivery speed of 149.7 kph/93.0 mph. The left-hander has confessed to modelling his delivery technique on that of the Pakistan legend Wasim Akram.

The Gentleman's Game

Sledges

So much for the gentleman's game! Cricketers perhaps more than any other sportsmen take on-field banter to a whole new level. And sledging, or 'mental disintegration' as Steve Waugh called it, is now part and parcel of the fun.

Below are some of the all-time classics uttered by some of the greatest and sometimes sharpest cricketers in the game. Not for the easily offended...

W G Grace It could be argued that it all started with the great man when one day he refused to leave the wicket after being got out cheaply by a young bowler. When the youngster politely inquired as to why the great batsman wouldn't leave, he smartly replied, 'My dear boy the people have come here to watch me bat and not to watch you bowl, off you go.'

Ian Botham When Ian Botham took guard in an Ashes match, abrasive Aussie wicket-keeper Rodney Marsh greeted him by saying, 'So, how's your wife and my kids?'

Merv Hughes During the 1989 Lord's Test, Aussie paceman Merv Hughes taunted England batsman Robin Smith after he had played and missed by saying: 'You can't f***ing bat.' After despatching a Hughes delivery to the boundary, Smith quipped: 'Hey Merv, we make a fine pair – I can't f***ing bat and you can't f***ing bowl!'

Javed Miandad The colourful Hughes was also involved in a memorable exchange with Pakistan's Javed Miandad who called him 'a fat bus conductor' during the 1991 Test at Adelaide. 'Tickets please,' yelled Hughes after dismissing Miandad a few balls later.

Merv Hughes (again!) During a test match in the West Indies, Hughes didn't say a word to Viv Richards once he came into bat, but continued to stare at him after deliveries. Eventually, Viv said, 'This is my island, my culture. Don't you be staring at me. In my culture we just bowl.'

Merv didn't reply, but after he dismissed him, he announced to the batsman, 'In my culture we just say f**k off.'

Daryll Cullinan When South Africa's Daryll Cullinan was on his way to the wicket, Aussie spinner Shane Warne told him he had been waiting for two years to humiliate him. 'Looks like you spent it eating,' Cullinan retorted.

Shaun Pollock After going past the outside edge of Ricky Ponting's bat with a couple of deliveries, South Africa bowler Shaun Pollock helpfully told the Aussie ace: 'It's red, round and weighs about five ounces.' After hammering the next ball out of the ground, Ponting turned to Pollock and said: 'You know what it looks like, now go and find it.'

Glenn McGrath The world-class Aussie fast bowler sent down another bullet to chicken-farmer-turned-cricketer Eddo Brandes and, as the rotund Zimbabwean played and missed yet again, McGrath thought it time to get basic. 'Oi Brandes, why are you so bloody fat?' said McGrath.

'Because every time I f**k your wife she gives me a biscuit!' was the rapid reply, sending each Aussie fielder into hysterics.

Ian Healy There has never been any love lost between the Australians and the Sri Lankans and especially between Ian Healy and the former Sri Lankan captain Arjuna Ranatunga. So when Ranatunga asked if he could get a runner during a One-Day match against Australia, Healy couldn't resist a cheeky pop at the roly-poly skipper saying, 'You don't get a runner in this game for being an unfit, overweight fat c**t!'

Cricketing Colemanballs

Live sports coverage often produces moments when commentators wish they had taken heed of the following advice: 'Engage brain before opening mouth.'

Perhaps the most famous of the lot. As England's Peter Willey prepared to face West Indies paceman Michael Holding, legendary

THE GENTLEMAN'S GAME

BBC radio commentator **Brian Johnston** uttered the immortal line: 'The batsman's Holding, the bowler's Willey.'

Johnners was involved in another memorable incident when he was in the commentary box with **Jonathan Agnew**, discussing the day's play. Agnew's comment that Ian Botham 'just didn't quite get his leg over' had his colleague in tears of laughter. 'Aggers, for goodness' sake, stop it,' pleaded Johnners as he struggled to compose himself.

On another occasion, **Agnew** told *Test Match Special* listeners: 'The truly marvellous thing about being up here in the commentary box is that you get a lovely view of Mushtaq's googlies.'

Ian Chappell told Channel 9 viewers in Australia: 'Fast bowlers are quick, even at the end of the day. Just watch this – admittedly it's in slow motion.'

As a player edged towards a century, pundit **Trevor Bailey** observed: 'He's on 90, ten away from that mythical figure.'

Bailey got himself in a tangle again when discussing the England captaincy. He said: 'The obvious successor to Brearley at the moment isn't obvious.'

Former BBC TV presenter **Peter West** once announced: 'And we have just heard, although this is not the latest score from Bournemouth, that Hampshire have beaten Nottinghamshire by nine wickets.'

Gaffe-prone commentator **David Coleman** got in on the act when he said: 'The Test match begins in ten minutes – that's our time, of course.'

One-time *Grandstand* presenter **Frank Bough** was going through a round-up of the latest scores when he said: 'After their 60 overs, West Indies have scored 244 for 7, all out.'

Quotes

Professional cricketers can often play a good game, but they can talk one too. Or can they?

'There has to be a very serious dilemma about representing your country on the cricket field in a land where people are suffering so much at the hands of their government.'
Mike Gatting talks about the England team's 2004 visit to Zimbabwe – could it be the same Mike Gatting who once took a rebel tour South Africa? Yes.

'If something happens, Michael, and you lead a side out there and someone gets killed, it will tarnish English cricket and your name for a long while.'
Nasser Hussain advises Michael Vaughan that he must accept a lot of responsibility captaining England in Zimbabwe during the same tour.

'My family called me Bunny because I ate lots of carrots.'
What's up **Nasser**?

THE GENTLEMAN'S GAME

'I admit I am selfish.'
Maybe that's why **Nasser** ate all those carrots.

'He'd say one thing one day and then suddenly he'd be saying that the same bloke he had been pushing for a year was now complete rubbish.'
Nasser Hussain questions Ian Botham's ability as a selector.

'The whole Zimbabwe fiasco was a low point for world cricket, the ICC and the ECB. All that happened was a complete shemozzle.'
Has **Nasser** been at the carrots again?

'Without a massive amount of pace on this tour we've got to look at other ways to skin the cat, and there's not a lot, to be honest.'
New Zealand captain **Stephen Fleming** doesn't fancy his side's chances against the Aussies.

'I am not going to be doing victory laps with four-for against that particular New Zealand side.'
Aussie spinner **Stuart MacGill** doesn't rate the Kiwis either.

'I've got no idea who I'm playing for tomorrow ... but it doesn't really matter; the point is I'm here and I am having an interesting experience.'
Australian player **Colin Miller** has a spell in an unpredictable American professional league.

'Sometimes, people think it's like polo, played on horseback, and I remember one guy thought it was a game involving insects.'
American cricketer **Clayton Lambert** says his fellow countrymen are not all keen on the game.

'I hope they can learn something – but I am not sure that they will.'
Ricky Ponting thinks America doesn't belong in big-time cricket.

'Why's that guy leaving? He can't just go – is he fed up with it?'
America's tennis star **Venus Williams** proves a point when watching a wicket tumble in a rare visit to a cricket match.

'Sachin was so focused. He never looked like getting out. He was batting with single-minded devotion. It was truly remarkable. It was a lesson.'
Czech-turned-American **Martina Navratilova** gets the point after watching Sachin Tendulkar during a break in the Australian Open tennis tournament.

'While you are riding the board you don't want to come crashing off and end up chewing sand.'
It's a good job New Zealand's **John Bracewell** is not responsible for explaining the intricacies of cricket to Americans.

'Thank God for the thriving DVD piracy trade on the sub-continent is about all I can say.'
Kiwi **Mark Richardson** finds something positive about playing in Bangladesh.

'I don't want the guys to be scared of failing. I want them to fail. Life is about failing. It's the way you learn.'
South Africa coach **Ray Jennings** does not expect to win much in his new job.

THE GENTLEMAN'S GAME

'If the players expect soft drinks, I will make sure there are none.
They will go to a tap and get on their knees and drink water until
they realise that it is an honour to play for their country.'
Ray Jennings tells it straight.

'I think there are a couple of players who need their butts
kicked.'
It's only a game, **Ray**.

'When Justin Langer finds his off stump akimbo he leaves the
crease only after asking the met office whether any earthquakes
have been recorded in the region. In any case, he never edges the
ball. It's just that his bat handle keeps breaking.'
Player-turned-reporter **Peter Roebuck** reveals that some players
wait until they are given out by the umpire before walking back to
the dressing room.

'The umpire has a job to do. I will wait for his decision.'
Mohammad Kaif explains that he doesn't want to put umpires out
of a job.

'Medical investigations have revealed intra-articular pathology of
the right hip joint noted by increased synovial fluid accumulation.'
We think **Sourav Ganuguly** has a bad back!

'If there was no television, there would be no huddle on a cricket
ground.'
Windies bowler **Michael Holding** thinks some players are show-
offs.

'I wouldn't like to spend time in an Indian jail if I am innocent.'
Does this mean **Herschelle Gibbs** wouldn't mind going to prison elsewhere if he hasn't done anything wrong?

'If he'd fielded at slip off his own bowling, he'd probably have 130 by now.'
Shane Warne takes his 99th Test catch, but team-mate **Mark Taylor** reckons he could have more.

'It's a team game, but when you get an individual record like that it's a pretty major one, so hopefully I can get it this game. Otherwise, I'd be pretty frustrated by the end of the five days. I'll be jumping off the nearest bridge.'
Do you think **Shane Warne** is keen to break a bowling record?

'Nothing against Indian food and all that, but I get sick over here. Hopefully, I'm better prepared this time. I've got my protein shakes, a few tins of spaghetti, a few tins of beans, I've got some cereal. Some people don't like seafood, I just don't like curries.'
Shane Warne launches his new diet.

'Sachin Tendulkar is, in my time, the best player without doubt – daylight second, Brian Lara third.'
Shane Warne's top three.

'Trescothick should go back to Somerset and learn how to play again.'
Marcus Trescothick did not make **Warne's** top three.

THE GENTLEMAN'S GAME

'I can categorically state that Shane did not say anything inappropriate about my mother.'
Either **Ronnie Irani's** mother is a 'whore', or Shane Warne was misreported.

'Maybe I was a little bit excited, as in eight previous matches I never bowled against him before, and I am sorry I hit him.'
Shoaib Akhtar says sorry to Lara.

'As long as Shoaib doesn't hit me again, a couple more years.'
Brian Lara predicts he will play on for a bit.

'I wanted to get back up and bop him on the chin.'
Gareth Batty explains what it's like to watch Lara hit his 400th run off his bowling.

'Brian Lara has had the great misfortune to be captaining the West Indies at their lowest ebb. Captain Ahab couldn't stop this ship from sinking.'
Lara does not have it all his way, according to **Michael Atherton**.

'Any time the West Indies lose, I cry.'
Lara's reign has been the cause of some concern to fellow countryman **Lance Gibbs** too.

'We're playing against Bangladesh and I'm not going to write off Bangladesh. The way we're playing right now you can't write off anybody at all.'
A new low point for **Brian Lara** and his team.

'I am not saying the players will get any better – but they can't become any worse.'
Colin Croft is not convinced.

'Corey Collymore and Adam Sanford wouldn't bowl my mum out.'
Either the West Indies bowlers really are useless, or **Geoffrey Boycott's** mother is handy with a bat.

'I'll tell you what pressure is. Pressure is a Messerschmitt up your arse. Playing cricket is not.'
Keith Miller reckoned the likes of Lara have nothing to worry about.

'If you get Dravid, great. If you get Sachin, brilliant. If you get Laxman, it's a miracle.'
Aussie bowler **Brett Lee** rates Indian batsmen.

'Steve Waugh once said that 'If we get Laxman, it's a miracle'.'
OK – we get your point, **Brett**.

'We are not vigilantes, we are not holding people to ransom.'
Kiwi **Chris Cairns** on reports that some players charge for an autograph.

'Please don't make me out to be a cad.'
Former pro **Mark Nicholas** hopes reports on his private life won't damage his reputation.

THE GENTLEMAN'S GAME

'Maybe they should try looking on E-Bay.'
Clare Skinner reacts to reports of a batch of umpire coats being stolen.

'He's not there much at the moment, he's usually out in the middle.'
Andrew Flintoff has little influence in the England dressing room, according to captain **Michael Vaughan**.

'But I do know I've drunk them all.'
Freddie Flintoff reveals why he can't remember how many Man-of-the-Match champagne awards he has won.

'We can win games without Andrew Flintoff and we will win games without Andrew Flintoff.'
There is more to English cricket than Andrew 'Freddie' Flintoff, says **Michael Vaughan**.

'She said that I wasn't quite right at the moment.'
Even HM The Queen reckons there is something wrong with **Freddie**.

'I'm not a fan of that sort of stuff. It's hard enough for the umpires to concentrate on what's going on without a lot of things going off in their ears.'
Ricky Ponting says that there is enough sledging for umpires to listen to without having to take on ear pieces as well.

'There must surely be young wicket-keepers in India, hiding somewhere, waiting to come out.'
It sounds as though **Farokh Engineer** wants to play hide n' seek.

'When people say I'm a sub-continental specialist, I say it's nice to be special at something.'
It's not only **Michael Kasprowicz's** mum who reckons he's special.

'Cut it off, lad – you've got a Test match to win.'
Graham Thorpe gets some medical advice on his fractured finger from fellow English batsman **Geoff Boycott**.

'*Test Match Special* is all chocolate cakes and jolly japes, but I didn't enjoy being called a wheelie-bin, and nor did my family.'
Ashley Giles responds to comments by Henry Blofeld.

'He has certainly left wheelie-binnery far behind.'
Legendary commentator **Henry Blofeld** believes Giles has improved, after all.

'Every dog has its day.'
Ashley Giles expands on his improvement.

'I don't know what they are trying to tell us, but it looks like they are expecting things to end early.'
West Indies manager **Tony Howard's** reaction when England handed him tickets for only the first four days of their Test match.

'We never give more than a one-year contract – it makes 'em soft.'
Lancashire League club chairman **Graham Tindall** takes a leaf out of Ray Jennings' book when it comes to overseas players.

'We know that we worked hard and put in one hundred per cent effort in this game. We will put in one hundred and fifty per cent effort on Friday and see what we can come up with.'
Mahela Jayawardene has a unique mathematical plan to stun Australia.

'They are rubbish wickets really.'
Do you think Kiwi international **Scott Styris** thinks there is a problem with English wickets?

'One-Day cricket is dead and buried for me now. It would be a huge backward step for England to pick me again.'
Graham Thorpe resists a call to come out of One-Day retirement.

'He keeps chucking me the ball, which is an absolute pain in the arse.'
Darren Lehmann on what it's like playing for Yorkshire when the captain happens to be brother-in-law Craig White.

'We found Rob Nicol, the Auckland batsman, on the terraces this afternoon, luckily before he went to the bar.'
John Bracewell on finding a substitute fielder to play in a Test against England.

'Boy George would be considered straight at the University of Western Australia.'
Kerry O'Keeffe doesn't like the results of the tests that cleared Muttiah Muralitharan's controversial 'chucking' action.

'I was brought up to be wary of people who pick up their bat and go home. Muralitharan has played all these Tests and taken all these cheap wickets, like against the Zimbabwe 2nd XI, but now he is not fronting up when the going gets tough.'
Nor does **Dennis Lillee**.

'I think he should just grow up, get on with it and go out there and play.'
Ditto **Shane Warne**.

'The game's leading wicket-taker is one of the great masters in Shane Warne, and hard on his heels is a burglar, a thief, a dacoit.'
Bishan Bedi enters the debate.

'I just want some quiet time, sit up there especially with Flem and Nathan, have a few drinks and talk garbage.'
Chris Cairns on his retirement plans.

'Generally the people out on the pitch are the ones who know how to play the game, not the people who are writing about it.'
Sounds as if **Marcus Trescothick** will not be reading this.

'If I had my time over again, I would never have played cricket. Why? Because of people like you. The press do nothing but criticise.'
Nor will **Sir Gary Sobers**.

'Well, that's fine – there is a record of ten others that are worse, or twelve others that are worse.'
Zimbabwe chairman **Peter Chingoka** takes a positive from two of the worst defeats in Test cricket.

THE GENTLEMAN'S GAME

'My personal opinion is that we would prefer them not to go. But there is a difference between doing that and ordering them not to go, which I think would step over the proper line. I think many people, however, believe – I think rightly – that the problem actually resides with the ICC.'
Tony Blair takes a lead on the Zimbabwe situation – NOT.

'I feel domestic cricket is tougher than international cricket. All you need to do is spend some time in the middle and runs will automatically come.'
International cricket comes easy to Pakistan's Asim Kamal

'The achievement that this team has achieved is a fantastic achievement.'
Michael Vaughan sounds like an overachiever.

'The celebrations out there are unbelievable and my mate Wayne Daniel is under the table.'
Matthew Hoggard's hat-trick against the West Indies causes Tony Greig and co. some excitement

'There's nothing wrong with being aggressive – the bloke down the other end has a bat, some pads and a helmet.'
England bowler Simon Jones gets ready to dig in a few short balls.

'It's all to do with meat ... you get a lot of aggression from beef and red meat.'
Pakistani coach Aaqib Javed has a theory on fast bowlers such as Jones.

'Virender Sehwag is a player of paranormal ability.'
Navjot Sidhu on Sehwag's big six to bring up a triple century.

'You expect a bit of chin music when you come to these parts.'
Michael Vaughan on playing in the West Indies.

'We have a nineteenth-century ground which we are required to bring into the twenty-first century of safety compliance. Somehow, the twentieth century passed us by.'
Sussex chairman **David Green** fears his championship-winning ground is in a time warp.

'Arjuna is probably slotting himself around at 150 kilos at the moment. Probably swallowed a sheep or something like that.'
Shane Warne assesses the size of Sri Lanka's Arjuna Ranatunga.

'It is better to swallow a sheep or a goat than swallow what he has been swallowing.'
Ranatunga hits back.

'There's nothing like putting your bare feet into fresh cow dung on a cold day. It's great.'
South Africans know how to enjoy themselves says **Makhaya Ntini**.

'I'd much rather be known as a great guitar player than a great batsman.'
Great batsman **Mark Butcher** will be disappointed.

'It probably dates back to the 60s and 70s when we scored about one win a decade and then spent the next decade celebrating it.'
Coach **John Bracewell** on the history of New Zealand cricket.

'I'm not sure how many people will play cricket once they have experienced the emotion of driving a sled down a huge track.'
There is no future for cricket according to India's sole winter Olympian **Shiva Keshavan**.

'We have enough players in our squad here who can hit the ball over the ropes. So, hopefully, at some stage there will be a role there for a nudger and nurdler like me. It's not a glamorous role, but it is there.'
England's **Andrew Strauss** knows his place.

Paying the Penalty

From indiscretions on the field to match-fixing scandals, cricket, for a game supposed to epitomise fair play, has had more than its share of disciplinary problems over the years.

Hansie Cronje

The former South Africa captain was banned from cricket for life in 2000 having admitted that he fixed matches after receiving money from bookmakers. He was killed in a plane crash two years later.

Saleem Malik
The Pakistan batsman was found guilty of match fixing in 2000 and handed a life-time ban from cricket. He has continued to protest his innocence, but several court appeals against the ban have failed.

Mohammad Azharuddin
The Indian Test star was banned for life in 2000 after being found guilty of match fixing. He admitted to fixing three One-Day internationals.

Ajay Sharma, Manoj Prabhakar & Ajay Jadeja
Azharuddin's team-mates Ajay Sharma, Manoj Prabhakar and Ajay Jadeja also received bans. Batsman Sharma was banned for life while all-rounders Prabhakar and Jadeja were suspended for five years.

Ed Giddins
In May 2004, Ed Giddins was banned from playing in any match under the jurisdiction of the England Cricket Board (ECB) for five years. He was found guilty of placing a bet of around £7,000 on his county Surrey losing to Northamptonshire in a National League game in August 2002. The former England bowler was also fined £5,000 plus £1,000 costs.

Mark Waugh & Shane Warne
The two players were fined by the Australian Cricket Board (ACB) in 1995 for providing information to an Indian bookmaker during Australia's tour of Sri Lanka the previous year. The ACB covered up the scandal until 1998 and did not reveal the size of

the fines, although reports allege Waugh was fined AUS $10,000 and Warne received an AUS $8,000 fine.

Andre Nel
The South African fast bowler was fined and suspended for six matches in 2003 after admitting to drink driving. He was fined his match fees from South Africa's tour of Australia, amounting to SA $2,248.

Shaun Pollock
South Africa's Shaun Pollock was fined his entire match fee for showing dissent during a One-Day international against Pakistan in 2003. Umpire Darrell Hair reported Pollock after he showed dissent following the rejection of an appeal during the match.

Virender Sehwag
The India batsman was fined 65 per cent of his match fee after being found guilty of misconduct during the first Test against Australia in 2004. Sehwag exchanged words with umpire Billy Bowden after being given out LBW off Glenn McGrath.

Mohammad Rafique
The Bangladesh spinner was fined half his match fee for showing excessive aggression against England's Mark Butcher during the second Test at the M A Aziz Stadium, in 2003.

Bad Hair Day

Cricketers are not the most glamorous bunch and do not compare to their footballing relatives when it comes to following, or starting, the latest fashions. Sometimes, they have made the mistake of trying to express themselves in the form of a hair cut – usually with disastrous results.

Ian Botham sported a bleached mullet in the mid 80s. At the time, he was represented by flamboyant entrepreneur Tim Hudson who dubbed him the 'new Errol Flynn' and had visions of helping the legendary all-rounder crack Hollywood. But the hairstyle did not last and Botham not surprisingly failed to forge an acting career.

On England's 1982–83 tour of Australia, **Graeme Fowler** befriended a Melbourne hairdresser, who persuaded him and two colleagues – **Derek Pringle** and **Ian Gould** – to have highlights put in their hair.

Following David Beckham's and some other fey footballer's lead, Lancashire and England ace **Dominic Cork** has taken to wearing an Alice band to keep his hair out of his eyes.

At least Lancashire and England fast bowler **James Anderson** had the decent excuse of being an Arsenal supporter when he had a red streak put in his hair. The proud football fan employed his Aunt Caroline to apply the colour, making him a dead ringer for Gunners midfielder Freddie Ljungberg.

Bob Willis's mop of curly brown hair tumbling over his collar was a familiar sight as he charged in to bowl for England in the 70s and 80s. But just because he was named after Bob Dylan, it doesn't mean he had to try and look like the tousle-haired hippy.

THE GENTLEMAN'S GAME

Former Australia spinner **Colin Miller** frequently changed his hair colour, once memorably dying it electric blue, but Aussie coach John Buchanan was not a fan, dismissing Miller's fashion statement as 'completely inappropriate'.

Miller's team-mate, **Damian Fleming**, also incurred the wrath of coach Buchanan. Fleming's flowing locks were said by Buchanan to be 'so long, they made him look like a girl'.

Ryan Sidebottom's hair is long, curly and ginger. 'Nuff said, bar that few, if any, cricketers, have chosen to copy the Nottinghamshire bowler's style.

Former England skipper **Graham Gooch** decided to follow in the footsteps of **Elton John** when he was faced with a receding hairline by having his scalp thatched.

Ex-Aussie spinner **Greg Matthews** underwent the same 'hair replacement' treatment as Gooch. When Matthews was on tour with Australia in England in 1986–87, he had his hair spiky.

Australia's **Jason Gillespie** has what can only be described as a classic mullet. He is Australian, which partly explains the style problem, but he is also a big fan of heavy metal music and clearly likes to blend in with other long-haired types when indulging in his passion.

It's Not Just Cricket

Cricketers are not often one-dimensional characters and have been known to turn their hand to more than just one sport or task. The following players certainly proved their sporting talents were not limited to the leather and willow.

J W H T Douglas As well as captaining England, Douglas also won a gold medal for Great Britain as a middle-weight boxer in the 1908 Olympics.

Denis & Leslie Compton The Compton brothers both played for Middlesex and England at cricket and played professional football too. They starred for Arsenal and were also capped by England.

David Acfield The ex-Essex spinner was heavily involved in fencing, but not of the criminal kind. Swash-buckling Acfield appeared in the 1968 and 1972 Olympics in his other sport.

Alistair Hignell As well as playing cricket for Gloucestershire, Hignell also played rugby union for Bristol and England.

M J K Smith Another England cricketer who played with the oval ball. He captained his country at both cricket and rugby union.

Ian Botham The legendary England all-rounder made eleven league appearances for Scunthorpe United Football Club between 1979–84.

Tony Cottey Before embarking on a successful career with Glamorgan and Sussex, Cottey was on the books of Swansea City FC and made a handful of appearances in their midfield.

Ted Dexter The ex-England batsman was a gifted amateur golfer who won the Oxford and Cambridge President's Putter on three occasions.

Keith Brown The former Middlesex wicketkeeper once had a promising boxing career and was also picked to play rugby for Essex.

Vince Clarke Before playing county cricket for Derbyshire, Clarke represented Western Australia as a pitcher in softball.

David Fulton The Kent batsman was a top ten UK table tennis player as a junior.

He Must Be on Drugs

Young men with far too much time and money on their times partaking in illegal and/or recreational drug use? Never

Ed Giddins
The one-time England bowler tested positive for cocaine in 1996, receiving an eighteen-month ban and a sacking from Sussex. A colourful character off the pitch, Giddins was ultimately kicked out of cricket for five years for placing a bet on his county to lose a match.

Ian Botham
England's greatest all-rounder was banned for a year in 1986 after

being found guilty of using cannabis. In his Test recall at The Oval he took the two dismissals he required to pass Dennis Lillee's then world record of 355 Test wickets.

Shane Warne

The Australian spinner was banned for a year in February 2003 after a drugs test found traces of a banned diuretic in his sample. 'My mother gave me a diet tablet. I'm shocked and absolutely devastated,' said the record-breaking Australian. As a result of his mistake, Warne was forced to miss the 2003 Cricket World Cup.

South Africa

In May 2001, five members of the South African team and their physiotherapist Craig Smith were found guilty of taking cannabis following their fourth Test victory against the West Indies. The guilty group included Herschelle Gibbs, Paul Adams, Roger Telemachus, Andre Nel and Justin Kemp. They were all each fined £887 as a result.

New Zealand

In 1994, New Zealand's Dion Nash, Stephen Fleming and Matthew Hart were accused of smoking cannabis. All three players received a three-match ban. Fleming, in particular, has put his youthful misdemeanours behind him and now leads the Black Caps with maturity and distinction.

Duncan Spencer

Western Australian fast bowler Spencer was banned for eighteen months in 2001 after testing positive for the banned steroid nandrolone. At the age of 29, he claimed he was taking a prescription to ease chronic back pain.

Graeme Rummans
New South Wales and Victoria player Rummans was banned for a month, and fined AUS $2000 in February 2002 after a drugs test revealed traces of the banned substance probenecid, a masking agent.

Graham Wagg
Twenty-one-year-old Warwickshire all-rounder Graham Wagg received a fifteen-month ban after testing positive for cocaine in October 2004. The former England A player was sacked by his county after unfortunately being tested following the 'first time' he'd tried it.

Paul Smith
Warwickshire all-rounder Paul Smith was handed a 22-month ban in 1996 after he admitted in a Sunday newspaper article publicising his book that he used cocaine and ecstasy during his career.

Keith Piper
Following Smith's admission, Warwickshire decided to test all their players. First-choice wicket-keeper Keith Piper was fined £500 and banned for one match when his test revealed traces of cannabis.

Famous Supporters

Celebrity supporters are often picked out during the televised coverage of sporting events. The following well-known personalities like to relax by watching cricket…

Lyricist **Sir Tim Rice** was made President of the MCC in 2002. His deep interest in cricket also saw him form his own team called the Heartaches.

Newscaster **Sir Trevor McDonald** is a keen cricket follower. He is a member of Surrey County Cricket Club and has written biographies of legendary West Indies duo Sir Viv Richards and Clive Lloyd

Chat show host **Michael Parkinson** lists cricket as one of his hobbies. He organises an annual Celebrity XI charity cricket match at Bray and Maidenhead cricket ground.

Impersonator **Rory Bremner** is among the celebrities who turn out for the Bunbury charity cricket team.

Other members of **David English's** merry Bunbury band have included musicians **Bill Wyman**, who has batted with a cigarette on the go, **Sir Elton John**, **Eric Clapton**, **David Essex** and **Barry Gibb**, comedians **Ronnie Barker**, **John Cleese**, topless models **Samantha Fox** and **Melinda Messenger**, actress **Joanna Lumley**, and England footballers **Gary Lineker** and **Ian Wright**.

THE GENTLEMAN'S GAME

Former Prime Minister **John Major's** love of cricket is well known. He was made President of Surrey CCC in 2000.

Mick Jagger, lead singer of the Rolling Stones, watches a lot of cricket. He bought the audio rights from the Sharjah Trophy cricket tournament in the United Arab Emirates, so that he could get coverage over the Internet.

Comedy actor **Tim Brooke-Taylor**, who starred in *The Goodies*, wrote a humorous book on the game called *Tim Brooke-Taylor's Cricket Box*.

One of Britain's best-known TV and stage actors, **David Troughton**, is a passionate cricket fan whose boyhood hero was West Indies legend Sir Gary Sobers.

BBC weather man **John Kettley** is a lifelong cricket fan. He rates Trent Bridge as his favourite cricket ground.

Legendary American actor **Robert Redford** became fascinated by the intricacies of cricket while working in England on the film *A Bridge Too Far*.

American tennis players **Venus Williams** and **Martina Navratilova** have both attended cricket matches games in between tennis matches in Australia.

Slang

The rules of cricket are complicated enough for some people, but what about the language! Cricket followers have their own terminology for all sorts of things. Here are some examples of the weird and wonderful terms used in the game:

Bosie: This is another name the Aussies use for a googly – why do they have to be different? Named after English cricketer B J T Bosanquet who perfected the art.

Bouncer: As ugly as the 'security staff' of the same name employed by nightclubs. A quick, short delivery, forcing the batsman to take evasive action.

Buffet bowling: Bowling so poor the batsman can just help himself to fours and sixes. Avoid the cheese and pineapple chunks on sticks.

A Bunsen: Not the metal object used in school chemistry labs but the term for a pitch that is spinners friendly, i.e. dry and dusty. A bunsen burner (turner) is a deck to make Ashley Giles look like Shane Warne. 'C'mon Gilo you've got a raging bunsen here!'

Chin music: The West Indian term for a barrage of short-pitched balls, usually followed up with the cry: 'Let 'im sniff de leather man!'

Chinaman: Not to be confused with Charlie Chan – a left-handed bowler's googly to a right-handed batsman.

THE GENTLEMAN'S GAME

The corridor: Term invented by England batting legend Geoffrey Boycott who suggested 'the corridor of uncertainty' was the perfect place for a bowler to bowl because the batsman had to play at the ball, but didn't know whether to play forward or back. Really, it just meant a good ball short of a length.

Feather: The faintest of edges from a batsman – often resulting in being caught behind.

Flipper: A technique employed by one of those crafty leg-spinners – an underhand delivery which comes at the batsman faster than a standard ball, with backspin.

Gardening: Nothing to do with Alan Titchmarsh or his cronies. It is when a batsman prods down loose areas of the pitch with the end of his bat.

Googly: Sounds rude, but it is an off-break ball bowled with apparent leg-break action.

Jaffa: A sweet, juicy bit of bowling – an unplayable delivery – not so effective when a piece of fruit is used.

Michelle 'Pfeifer': A play on the Hollywood star's surname, as in 'I picked up a cheeky Michelle today' – 'five for'

Rib tickler: A short-pitched ball that is aimed at the heart and if the bowler's lucky will find its way to the batsman's rib cage. As Aussie quickie Brett Lee said, 'Just like a dagger to the heart, mate!'

Sledging: Having a go at an opponent in an attempt to unsettle him, usually by way of a barrage of expletives. Also known as 'mental disintegration' according to Aussie legend Steve 'should we put a bell in it for ya' Waugh.

Wrong 'Un: An Australian term for a googly.

Bizarre Injuries

All sportsmen find it difficult to deal with long spells on the sidelines, especially when injured and unable even to train, but it's even worse when the reason for the absence causes amusement among teammates and spectators alike.

1. Steve Harmison
England captain Nasser Hussain thought he'd help out his giant fast bowler by marking out a fielding spot with his heal. Harmison consequently sprained his ankle when he tripped over the divot made by his helpful skipper. Harmy also once aggravated an old back injury by turning around on a plane to grab a pen and piece of paper with his seat belt still on.

2. Ian Greig
Tony's younger brother Ian won two England caps as an all-rounder, but was also rather injury prone. He broke his ankle when he fell 18 feet, attempting to break into his own house after he snapped his key off in the front-door lock.

Later in his career Greig was hit on the finger while batting and went to hospital for the x-ray which revealed the break. As he got up he banged his head on the machine and subsequently needed two stitches in his forehead.

3. Phil Edmonds
Born in Zambia, then Northern Rhodesia, to an English father and Belgian mother, Edmonds was a talented slow left-arm spinner who found himself deputising for Derek Underwood for most of his career. However 'deadly Derek' remained in pole position after Edmonds' injured his back getting out of his car at Lord's.

4. Paul Collingwood
The happy-go-lucky England all-rounder, and One-Day specialist, regularly displays his natural athleticism in the field, but unfortunately that ability doesn't extend to the basketball court. While getting a bit of training done on the court during the rain-hit West Indies tour, Collingwood rose like a salmon to claim a basket, but came down like a sack of spuds as he ran into the metal pole behind the net. Claret everywhere and his nose in two parts, sport hurts!

5. Steve Waugh & Jason Gillespie
Mine! No mine! Ouch! If in doubt, let someone else catch it – the policy that has served England so well over the years should have been adopted by the Aussies in 1999, at least it would have kept two of their players out of hospital. The Australian captain and his opening fast bowler collided while attempting to catch Mahela Jayawardene's skied drive in the first Test in Kandy, in 1999. The ugly clash resulted in a broken nose for Waugh and a broken leg for 'Dizzy'. With both men absent their teammates fell for 140 in the second innings, and Sri Lanka went on to win by six wickets.

6. Terry Alderman

Don't mess with this Aussie fast-medium bowler. He won't play around, as a streaker found out in 1982 when Alderman tackled the man and his tackle to the ground during the first innings of the Perth Test against England. However, Alderman was to pay the ultimate price for his bravery as he missed more than a year of international cricket after badly damaging his shoulder in the act and had to reinvent himself as a bowler following his injury.

7. Paul Downton

Downton had a tough task behind the stumps, following in the footsteps of Alan Knott and Bob Taylor for England. He was a useful and determined batsman, but occasionally marred capable wicket-keeping performances by missing a vital chance. His career was ended prematurely after a bail struck him in the left eye during a Sunday League match for Middlesex in 1990 impairing his vision.

8. Derek Pringle

Pringle received a surprise promotion to the England side in 1982, after captaining Cambridge University with distinction earlier that season. In four years at Cambridge the England seamer must have kept written work to a minimum, as he once injured his back while writing a letter on the eve of a Test match.

9. Gil Langley

Labour MP for Unley in the South Australian Parliament for twenty years, Langley preceded a career in politics by keeping wicket for state and country during the 1950s. He once missed a Test match because he damaged his hand in his sleep by lying on it.

10. Ted Dexter

A talented and versatile sportsman, Dexter was born in Milan, and made his name as a batting all-rounder, coming in at number three for England and Sussex. He had an extended spell on the sidelines after once breaking his leg when his own car ran him over.

Foot In Mouth Disease

Sometimes the pressure of the situation can get to a sportsman and they end up saying something they wish they hadn't, largely because it ends up biting them on the backside and making them look like idiots.

David 'Bumble' Lloyd is one of England's most well-loved characters in his role as a Sky Sports commentator and he has come up with many a gem behind the microphone. But it was in his job as England coach that he produced his most memorable line following a tied Test with Zimbabwe in 1996. The minnows of Test cricket took England to the wire and avoided the expected defeat – even though the result didn't go England's way, Lloyd still reckoned: 'We murdered em, We flippin murdered 'em.' Oh dear.

In 1976, the England cricket team were full of hope as they prepared for a home series against the West Indies, prompting captain Tony Greig to utter the now immortal words 'We'll make them grovel'. Unsurprisingly, the comment came back to haunt him when England were systematically butchered by a superb West Indian bowling attack and lost the series 3–0

Not shy of a comment or two, **Sir Viv Richards** was intrigued to see Indian opener Sunil Gavaskar come in at number four for a change during a match at Madras in 1983. Malcolm Marshall got Anshuman Gaekwad and Dilip Vengsarkar for ducks and the score was 0 for 2 when Gavaskar strolled to the wicket. Richards said: 'Man, it don't matter where you come in to bat, the score is still zero.' Gavaskar made 236.

Muttiah Muralitharan's bowling action has come in for more questions than your average politician, but with over 400 Test wickets to his name it looked like the worst was behind him, or at least that is what umpire **Ross Emerson** thought when he said, 'Muralitharan's action has changed since 1995 – it's got worse – but he's not worried about it because who's gonna call a bloke who's got more than 400 test wickets.

'I still consider his action illegal, as do most umpires around the world, but they won't do anything about it because they're worried about their jobs.' Funny how Murali was banned from using his 'doosra' in 2004 and then backed out of the tour to Australia (where he has been regularly branded a cheat) for 'personal reasons'.

The cricket world was lucky to have a man like **Hansie Cronje** in charge of South Africa. He was just the man to lead the rejuvenated nation to glory and would unite the whole nation behind him. So when he was accused of match fixing it all came as a bit of a shock. He said: 'The allegations are completely without substance. I have been privileged to play for South Africa since 1992 and I want to assure every South African I have made a hundred per cent effort to win every match that I have played.' Cronje later came clean over the whole affair that blew cricket wide apart. He was banned from the game for life and was killed in a plane crash in 2002.

On the Screen

Cricket Films

The gentleman's game entertains people throughout the world, whether at a ground, listening on the radio, or watching TV at home. But the game that lends itself so seamlessly to the small screen has yet to bring big numbers through the turnstiles of cinemas outside the Indian sub-continent.

Bodyline: It's not just Cricket (1984)
This film dramatises the 1932–33 Test series between England and Australia. The series marked itself in history following the England team's employment of a novel bowling technique known as 'bodyline'. This aggressive technique aroused hostility from the Aussies and plunged relations between the teams into turmoil.

Lagaan: Once Upon a Time in India (2001)
Members of a small Indian village are challenged to a game of cricket by their British rulers. The villagers will only be excused

from paying the hefty land taxes imposed by the British colonisers if they win the game. The villagers are unfamiliar with the game of cricket and only one brave soul is willing to take up the challenge. However, he must rally the support of his fellow villagers if he is to stand a chance of victory.

The Final Test (1953)

A cricket player prepares to play his last match before retiring. His son Jackson, an aspiring poet, is fearful that he will not be able to attend his father's last match. He is aware of the disappointment this will cause. High drama, of course.

Wondrous Oblivion (2003)

A young Jewish boy is able to indulge his love of cricket when a Jamaican family move into the neighbourhood, allowing the boy to practise their cricket net. A friendship is formed between the boy and the family, united by their shared passion for the sport. Set in 1950s London, however, issues of race throw the friendship into jeopardy.

Silence Please – The Dressing Room (2004)

A friendly cricket match between India and Pakistan is threatened when a terrorist group plan an attack on the stadium. Theories of corruption and match fixing threaten the unity of the Indian team. The police eventually foil the terrorists' plan and the film climaxes in the match. We all like a nice happy ending.

Trobriand Cricket: An Ingenious Response to Colonialism (1974)

Trobriand islanders exploit the game of cricket to make a political comment on the issue of colonialism. The sport, introduced by the missionaries, becomes a ritual for the islanders which diminishes the pain of the colonial experience.

Stumped (2003)
Parallelling the 1999 Cricket World Cup and the Kargil War, the film explores the power of a nation's obsession with cricket to distract it from more important social issues. The story revolves around a wife awaiting news from the army of her husband, as the local community remains mesmerised by the game of cricket.

P'tang Yang Kipperbang (1984)
An innocent romance between a boy and a girl. The boy parallels his own romantic dilemma with the plight of a cricket team, relating the match commentary to his own life. Who says it's only a game?

Outside Edge (1982)
The narrative revolves around a local cricket team captained by the enthusiastic Roger. The film explores the relationships within the team, focusing particularly on the role of the tea lady who is largely neglected by the rest of the team. Let that be a lesson to all those cricketing prima donnas – respect your tea lady. Without her, you'd have to make your own cup of tea. A must-see for tea ladies everywhere.

Anything For Money

Product endorsement can be a money-spinning sideline for some of the higher profile players and they will advertise anything and everything from hair products to motorbikes...

ON THE SCREEN

Stylish England batsman **Denis Compton** was known as the 'Brylcreem Boy' after being recruited to advertise the hair styling product. Compton's face and gleaming hair appeared on posters across the country, earning him a reported £1,000-a-year.

Ian Botham cashed in on his status as a sporting idol when he appeared on TV, advertising Shredded Wheat breakfast cereal – an advert still running today.

Pepsi is one of a number of products to have been endorsed by **Sachin Tendulkar**. The Indian Test ace has amassed a fortune after appearing in adverts promoting various brands, including Band-Aid, Gillette and Phillips.

Australian pair **Shane Warne** and **Brett Lee** have both promoted Fosters lager.

Warne was also recruited by a pharmaceutical company to promote Nicorette gum and patches. The deal was that he would receive a reported AUS $200,000 if he quit smoking in four months. Despite being caught puffing away just a few days before the end of the contract, he was allowed to keep the cash.

India's **Kapil Dev** was signed-up by motorcycle manufacturers Kinetic Engineering in his homeland to promote their range of two-wheelers. He has also been the face of Palmolive shaving cream.

Legendary Indian opener **Sunil Gavaskar** lent his name to clothing company Dinesh Suitings.

Migraine-suffering England batsman **Mark Butcher** endorses Migra-Cap. According to the promotional material, the stretchy lycra cap provides 'medication-free relief from the pain that is associated with migraine and most types of headaches'.

Former England skipper **Graham Gooch** and ex-Australia spinner **Greg Matthews** both promote the hair replacement company Advanced Hair Studio. 'Before and after' photos of the pair regularly appear in English newspaper adverts, showing their thinning locks apparently replaced by a full head of hair.

Poachers turned Gamekeepers

Former England captain David Gower once got so annoyed with the media in a post-match press conference that he picked up his drink and stormed out without a care for the reporters or their deadlines. Funnily enough, he loves the media now that he's one of them – and he's not the only one...

Press XI

Sunil Gavaskar The Indian Test legend is a columnist for the *Hindustan Times*. He is also chairman of the ICC cricket committee.

Mike Atherton After a degenerative back condition forced his retirement in 2001, Atherton decided to go into the media. He writes for the *Sunday Telegraph* and also commentates for Channel 4.

ON THE SCREEN

Jack Fingleton Australia's opening bat in the 1930s, Fingleton worked for the *Sydney Sun* and *Sydney Morning Herald* and was also cricket correspondent for newspapers in England, India and South Africa.

Lindsay Hassett The one-time Australia captain covered cricket for *The Sporting Globe*. He also worked in radio for ABC.

Keith Miller One of Australia's all-time greats, Miller wrote for the *Daily Express* for many years. He was also cricket correspondent of *The Herald* in his homeland and broadcast on TV and radio.

Peter Roebuck The former Somerset batsman, who now resides in Australia, writes for the *Sydney Morning Herald* and the *Daily Telegraph*.

Derek Pringle Following a career as a medium-pace bowler with Essex and England, the Cambridge graduate turned to journalism. He is the *Daily Telegraph*'s cricket correspondent.

Vic Marks The former Somerset and England spinner is the cricket correspondent of the *Observer*, and a much loved member of the Radio 4 *Test Match Special* commentary team.

Bill O'Reilly The great Aussie leg-spin bowler wrote for the *Sydney Morning Herald* for 42 years before his retirement in 1988. He was also the author of several books.

Angus Fraser After bringing the curtain down on his career, the former Middlesex and England bowler swapped the leather and willow for a laptop. He covers cricket for the *Independent*.

Simon Hughes Now a columnist for the *Daily Telegraph* after playing for Middlesex and Durham. He is also the author of a number of critically acclaimed books and a key broadcaster for Channel 4.

TV XI

Mark Nicholas Formerly captain of Hampshire, Nicholas has carved out a successful career as a TV presenter and anchors Channel 4's cricket coverage.

Nasser Hussain When Hussain decided to call time on his Essex and England career, his services were immediately snapped up by Sky Sports.

David Gower His laid-back style has enabled the former England captain to move effortlessly into TV presenting. Gower now hosts Sky's coverage of international cricket and was a team captain on BBC TV's *They Think It's All Over*.

Tony Lewis The former England captain graduated from the *Test Match Special* team to become the anchorman for the BBC television coverage of Test and domestic cricket.

David Lloyd 'Bumble' quit as England coach after the 1999 World Cup to join the Sky Sports commentary team, and his infectious enthusiasm has seen him dubbed the voice of Twenty20.

Ian Botham When he is not doing a charity walk, 'Beefy' is a regular member of the Sky Sports commentary team.

ON THE SCREEN

Dermot Reeve Now a TV pundit on Channel 4, following a playing career which took in Sussex and Warwickshire as well as earning him a few England caps to boot.

Richie Benaud The doyen of cricket broadcasters. Now with Channel 4 after working for the BBC for many years, first on radio and then TV. The former Aussie skipper also commentates for Channel 9 in his homeland.

Ian Smith The former New Zealand wicketkeeper now travels the world commentating on the game and is a regular on Channel 4.

Michael Holding Nicknamed 'Whispering Death' during his days as a fearsome fast bowler for the West Indies, Holding now commentates for various TV and radio stations.

Bob Willis Retired after taking 325 wickets for England and has worked as a commentator for Sky since 1992.

Radio XI

Geoff Boycott The straight-talking Yorkshireman has worked for various media organisations since hanging up his bat. His radio career has included spells working for the BBC and talkSPORT.

Chris Broad The ex-England opener became a freelance TV and radio commentator upon retirement, covering athletics and rugby as well as cricket. Later appointed an ICC match referee.

Mike Gatting He may be most remembered for arguing with umpire Shakoor Rana in Pakistan, but the former England captain and middle order batsman is earning an improving reputation as a member of the *Test Match Special* and Radio Five's commentary teams.

Greg Chappell Media work accounts for some of the former Australia skipper's time. Chappell commentates for the ABC radio station in his homeland.

Chris Cowdrey The former Kent and England all-rounder started his broadcasting career with the BBC before switching to talkSPORT.

Tony Greig Another member of the talkSPORT commentary team. The former England skipper also works for Australia's Channel 9 TV station.

Ian Healy The record-breaking Aussie wicketkeeper hung up his gloves for the microphone and together with Mark Taylor has become a firm favourite, commentating on both radio and TV.

Jack Bannister After a lengthy spell with the BBC, the former England bowler is the commentating anchorman for talkSPORT.

Fred Trueman 'Fiery Fred' was a member of the BBC's *Test Match Special* team for many years, playing the role of curmudgeonly Yorkshireman to perfection.

ON THE SCREEN

Mike Selvey Now combines his role as a *Test Match Special* commentator and cricket correspondent of the *Guardian* with other broadcasting work. He came charging in for Surrey, Middlesex, Glamorgan and England.

Jonathan Agnew A stalwart of the *Test Match Special* team since 1990, following a career as a fast bowler for Leicestershire and England.

Up for the Cup

World Cup Facts

The World Cup – the holy grail of cricket's One-Day game – is a relatively new addition to the sporting calendar and used to be held exclusively in England. Here are some of the heroes and villains of the competition.

England 1975
The first ball to be bowled in World Cup history was delivered by India's Madan Lal to England's Denis Amiss at Lord's on 7 June 1975.

India's opening batsman Sunil Gavaskar lasted the full 60 overs in the opening game against the hosts at Lord's, but scored only 36 runs.

England 1979
West Indies legend Viv Richard's 139 not out is the highest score in a World Cup Final.

Sri Lanka were the first nation to boycott a match in World Cup history when they refused to complete their fixture with Israel, on political grounds, in the group stage.

England 1983
Kapil Dev played one of the all-time great innings, but his dashing 175 against Zimbabwe was lost to posterity. Unfortunately for the great Indian all-rounder, the BBC were on strike that day and the game was not recorded.

Indian wicket-keeper Syed Kirmani achieved the most stumpings in a World Cup match with two against the West Indies.

India & Pakistan 1987
This World Cup saw the event move from England to the Indian sub-continent for the first time since the tournament began.

England's Graham Gooch became the only player to win three Man-of-the-Match awards consecutively.

India, Pakistan & Sri Lanka 1996
Mark Waugh of Australia is still the only player to hit three centuries in one World Cup Competition.

Sri Lanka were the first team to be awarded a match by default. In the semi-final between India and Sri Lanka at Eden Gardens crowd disturbances forced the match referee's decision.

England 1999
The semi-final between Australia and South Africa was deemed one of the finest One-Day matches ever and regarded by some as the real final of this tournament. Australia went on to win the title after a run of seven games without a single defeat.

South Africa 2003
Chaminda Vaas of Sri Lanka holds the record for taking the most wickets in a tournament with 23.

Indian Batsman Sachin Tendulkar holds the record for most runs, with 673 scored in his 11 innings.

Mohammad Kaif of India made the most catches in one game when he held four against Sri Lanka.

Australian Glenn McGrath holds the record of the most wickets taken in a single match with seven against Namibia.

More World Cup Facts and Records

Namibian **Ruud van Vuuren** became the first player to represent his country in both cricket and rugby union World Cups during 2003.

Wasim Akram of Pakistan holds the current record for most World Cup matches played with a total of 38 and also the most wickets taken with 55.

Unfortunate New Zealander **Nathan Astle** has scored the most World Cup ducks with five in 22 matches played.

Sachin Tendulkar of India has won the most Man-of-the-Match awards with eight in total and has hit the most runs with 1,732 in 33 World Cup matches.

UP FOR THE CUP

Indian captain **Mohammad Azharuddin** has led his country out 23 times in World Cup competitions and currently holds the record for the most appearances as skipper.

Saurav Ganguly and **Sachin Tendulkar**, both of India, share the record for the most centuries scored in World Cup matches with four each.

Australia's **Ricky Ponting** holds the record for the most catches in World Cup games with eighteen in 28 matches.

Pakistani **Javed Miandad** holds the world record of six World Cup finals appearances.

Sudath Pasqual of Sri Lanka became the youngest player to represent his country in the World Cup finals when he made his debut against New Zealand in 1979 at the age of just seventeen years and 238 days.

Dutchman **Nolan Clarke** became the oldest player to represent his country in the World Cup finals when he played against South Africa in 1996 at the age of 47 years and 258 days.

English umpire **David Shepherd** has appeared 46 times in World Cup finals spanning from his first outing in 1983 to his last in 2003 World Cup and he still currently holds the world record.

South African big hitter **Gary Kirsten** achieved the highest individual score in a World Cup match when he reached 188 against United Arab Emirates in 1996.

Indian pair **Saurav Ganguly** (183) and **Rahul Dravid** (145) reached a record high partnership of 318 against Sri Lanka in 1999.

C & G – One-Day Cup Facts

Way back in 1963 it was decided that the game needed a One-Day competition to liven things up a bit and so was born 'The Knock Out Cup'. Now known as the Cheltenham and Gloucester Trophy, cricket's equivalent of the FA Cup has had a successful history of competition.

* There were seventeen first-class counties taking part when the 65-over competition started in 1963. Sussex beat Worcestershire in the final and total prize money for the entire tournament totalled £6,500.

* A year later and the first-class counties were joined by five of the minor counties in the Cup. It was renamed the Gillette Cup after the arrival of a new sponsor and 60-over matches became the order of the day. Sussex retained their trophy.

* Gillette continued their sponsorship until 1980 and were replaced as title sponsors by Nat West Bank in 1981.

* Scotland joined the fray two years later, along with eight more minor counties. The emergence of Durham as a first-class side and the addition of Holland into the Cup has reduced the representation of minor counties to eleven.

UP FOR THE CUP

* Gloucestershire currently dominate the scene having won four out of the last six competitions.

Counties with the Most Wins

Lancashire	7
Warwickshire	5
Gloucestershire	5
Middlesex	4
Sussex	4
Somerset	3
Yorkshire	3
Essex	2
Kent	2
Northamptonshire	2
Nottinghamshire	1
Surrey	1
Derbyshire	1
Hampshire	1
Worcestershire	1
Durham	0
Glamorgan	0
Leicestershire	0

Role of Honour

YEAR	WINNERS	RUNNERS-UP	WINNING MARGIN
1963	Sussex	Worcestershire	14 runs
1964	Sussex	Warwickshire	8 wkts

1965	Yorkshire	Surrey	175 runs
1966	Warwickshire	Worcestershire	5 wkts
1967	Kent	Somerset	32 runs
1968	Warwickshire	Sussex	4 wkts
1969	Yorkshire	Derbyshire	69 runs
1970	Lancashire	Sussex	6 wkts
1971	Lancashire	Kent	24 runs
1972	Lancashire	Warwickshire	4 wkts
1973	Gloucestershire	Sussex	40 runs
1974	Kent	Lancashire	4 wkts
1975	Lancashire	Middlesex	7 wkts
1976	Northamptonshire	Lancashire	4 wkts
1977	Middlesex	Glamorgan	5 wkts
1978	Sussex	Somerset	5 wkts
1979	Somerset	Northamptonshire	45 runs
1980	Middlesex	Surrey	7 wkts
1981	Derbyshire	Northamptonshire	N'hants lost more wickets
1982	Surrey	Warwickshire	9 wkts
1983	Somerset	Kent	24 runs
1984	Middlesex	Kent	4 wkts
1985	Essex	Nottinghamshire	1 run
1986	Sussex	Lancashire	7 wkts
1987	Nottinghamshire	Northamptonshire	3 wkts
1988	Middlesex	Worcestershire	3 wkts
1989	Warwickshire	Middlesex	4 wkts
1990	Lancashire	Northamptonshire	7 wkts
1991	Hampshire	Surrey	4 wkts
1992	Northamptonshire	Lancashire	8 wkts
1993	Warwickshire	Sussex	5 wkts

UP FOR THE CUP

1994	Worcestershire	Warwickshire	8 wkts
1995	Warwickshire	Northamptonshire	4 wkts
1996	Lancashire	Essex	129 runs
1997	Essex	Warwickshire	9 wkts
1998	Lancashire	Derbyshire	9 wkts
1999	Gloucestershire	Somerset	50 runs
2000	Gloucestershire	Warwickshire	22 runs (Duckworth Lewis)
2001	Somerset	Leicestershire	41 runs
2002	Yorkshire	Somerset	6 wkts
2003	Gloucestershire	Worcestershire	7 wkts
2004	Gloucestershire	Worcestershire	8 wkts

In the Slips

If He's Good Enough ... The Oldest Test Players

Never let it be said that cricket is a young man's game. Well, it didn't used to be judging by this bunch of old-timers.

PLAYER	AGE	FOR	WHERE	WHEN
Rhodes, W	52y 165d	ENG v WI	Kingston	1930
Ironmonger, H	50y 327d	AUS v Eng	Sydney	1933
Grace, W G	50y 320d	ENG v Aus	Nottingham	1899
Gunn, G	50y 303d	ENG v WI	Kingston	1930
Southerton, J	49y 139d	ENG v Aus	Melbourne	1877
Miran Bux	47y 302d	PAK v Ind	Peshawar	1955
Hobbs, J B	47y 249d	ENG v Aus	The Oval	1930
Woolley, F E	47y 87d	ENG v Aus	The Oval	1934
Blackie, D D	46y 309d	AUS v En	Adelaide	1929
Strudwick, H	46y 202d	ENG v Aus	The Oval	1926

1. Wilfred Rhodes was a right-handed batsman who doubled up with an impressive left-handed leg spin. The Yorkshire all-rounder

went from playing number 11 in his debut Test against Australia at Trent Bridge in 1899 to opening the Test batting with Jack Hobbs. In his 58 Tests for England he scored 2,325 runs with a highest score of 179 and took 127 wickets with a best of 8 for 68. He was named Wisden Cricketer of the Year in 1899.

2. **Bert Ironmonger**, also known as Dainty, was a late starter when, against England at Brisbane in 1928, he made his Test debut at the age of 45 years and 237 days – making him the fourth oldest debutant in history. During his fourteen-Test career he took 74 wickets including four five-wicket innings – and achieved all this without the forefinger of his left hand.

3. **William Gilbert Grace**, known simply as W G, is responsible for turning cricket from just another sport into the great institution it is today. He was the first great champion of the game. His Test career included making over 10,000 runs with an average of 32.29 and claiming 239 wickets – including opening for England at the age of 50. With over 54,000 first-class runs, including 839 in just eight days in 1876, when he hit a couple of triple centuries and over 2,800 wickets he became recognised as the 'father' of the game.

4. **George Gunn** was probably the best ever batsman who turned out for Nottinghamshire. During his fifteen-match Test career he amassed a total of 1,120 runs at an average of 40.00 and he was voted Wisden's Cricketer of the Year in 1914. Gunn was also a remarkable slip fielder and it was there that he made the lion's share of his 438 catches.

5. James Southerton holds the record for the oldest Test debut at the ripe old age of 49 years and 119 days. His career spanned only two matches in which he got as many wickets as he did runs – a magnificent seven.

6. Miran Bux is the second oldest Test debutant but, as with James Southerton, didn't make up for lost time because he made only a couple of appearances in back-to-back Tests against India in 1954–55 in Lahore and Peshawar, but he did pick up two wickets in those Tests.

7. John Berry Hobbs, known as 'The Master' or simply 'Jack', is recognised as England's most prolific batsman with 61,237 first-class runs and was knighted for his services to cricket in 1953 – the first ever professional cricketer to receive the honour. He would have scored more but World War One intervened, as did Hobbs' tendency to get out soon after making a century 'to give some one else a go'. Half of all of his centuries came after he was 40 years old and he still remains the oldest man to make a Test century at the age of 64.

8. Frank Edward Woolley was one of best left-handed all-rounders ever and was noted for his elegant strokes, despite being well over six-feet tall, his perfect timing made him a joy to watch. In 64 Tests he amassed a total of 3,283 runs at an average of 36.07 as well as taking 83 wickets and making 64 catches. His first-class runs total of 58,969 is surpassed only by Sir Jack Hobbs and he holds the record for catches of 1,015 – the majority at slip.

9. **Donald Dearness Blackie** played only three matches for Australia and, aged 46, was the oldest player to play for his country. The right-handed off-break bowler took fourteen wickets in his three Tests at an average of 31.71 and with a best of 6-94.

10. **Bert Strudwick** held the world record for the most dismissals in a career by a wicket-keeper. His Test career spanned 28 matches and he took a total of 61 catches and made twelve stumpings. Struddy was one of the most popular players of his day and, as an honorary member of the MCC, has an oil painting of himself hanging in the Long Room to commemorate him.

If He's Good Enough ... The Youngest Ever Test Players:

Pakistan's **Hasan Raza** is the game's youngest ever Test player. He was fourteen years and 227 days old when he played in the match against Zimbabwe at Faisalabad in 1996.

Brian Close holds the record for being the youngest player to have appeared for England in a Test match. The Yorkshireman was eighteen years and 149 days old when he made his debut against New Zealand at Old Trafford in 1949.

India's **Nawab of Pataudi Jnr** is in the record books as the youngest Test captain. He played against West Indies at Bridgetown in 1961–62 at the age of 21 years and 77 days.

Monty Bowden is the youngest player to have captained England in a Test match. He was 23 years and 144 days old when he led the team against South Africa at Johannesburg on the 1888–89 tour.

The youngest century-maker in the history of Test cricket is **Mohammad Ashraful** of Bangladesh. When he hit a ton against Sri Lanka at Colombo in 2001, Ashraful was aged seventeen years and 63 days.

In June 1938, at the age of twenty years and 19 days, **Denis Compton** became England's youngest century maker when he scored 102 against Australia at Trent Bridge.

Sri Lanka spinner **Muttiah Muralitharan** became the youngest bowler in Test history to claim 400 wickets when he bowled Zimbabwe's Henry Olonga in January 2002 at the age of 29.

One of the greatest batsman of all time **Sachin Tendulkar** was given his Test debut at just sixteen years 205 days old in 1989, scoring his first Test century the following year. And at the age of ninteen years and 217 days he became the youngest Test cricketer to reach 1,000 runs.

One-Cap Wonders

The following band of players had only a fleeting taste of Test match action.

IN THE SLIPS

Sir Aubrey 'Round-the-Corner' Smith The Sussex-player-turned-Hollywood-actor uniquely captained England in his only Test which came against South Africa in 1888-89.

George Mudie His one Test, against England at Kingston in 1935, clinched the West Indies' first series win. He made a valuable contribution with the first of his three wickets breaking the sixth-wicket stand of 157 between Les Ames and Jack Iddon. But that was not enough to earn him another call-up.

Bal Dani The Indian all-rounder boasted a highly impressive record in the domestic game, but his Test career failed to get off the ground. His solitary appearance for India came against Pakistan at Bombay in 1952–53 when he took one wicket-but did not get to bat.

Ashley Woodcock A regular in the South Australia side for nine seasons, Woodcock made his only Test appearance for Australia against New Zealand in 1973–74. His form dropped alarmingly over the next couple of years and he was effectively finished by the time he was 30.

Alan Butcher A stylish left-hand opener who captained Surrey and Glamorgan, his only Test appearance for England came in 1979 against India at The Oval, where he scored 14 and 20.

Andy Lloyd The Warwickshire batsman's Test career lasted just 33 minutes. Facing the mighty West Indies at Edgbaston. in 1984, he was felled by a Malcolm Marshall bouncer and carried from the field. Lloyd never regained the form required to win a recall.

Mark Benson Opener Benson was unfortunate to play in just one Test – against India at Edgbaston, in 1986. The Kent left-hander made 30 and 21 and looked quite comfortable, but he failed to receive another call-up.

Simon Brown The left-arm, medium-fast bowler got off to a good start in the 1996 Test against Pakistan at Lord's, trapping Aamer Sohail LBW with his tenth ball. But the Durham player failed to make another appearance and he drifted out of the game at a relatively young age.

Best Captains

Some captains lead by example, turning in regular match-winning performances with the bat or ball. Others have the knack of being able to coax the best out of other, more naturally talented individuals. Due to their influence on selection and tactics, cricket captains are far more influential than skippers in nearly every other sport. Here is our selection of the game's finest leaders.

Douglas Jardine Widely recognised as one of England's best-ever captains, Jardine will forever be remembered for his role in the controversial 1932–33 'Bodyline' tour of Australia. He ordered his bowlers to bowl to a packed, leg-side field and the ploy worked with England winning four of the five Tests. But the Australians argued the tactics were against the spirit of the game.

Peter May The Surrey batsman captained England in a record 41 Tests. England won twenty of those Tests and lost only ten. He was an unchallenged figure of authority who later served his country again as chairman of selectors.

Ray Illingworth The Yorkshireman's time as England captain included an Ashes-winning tour. He was tactically astute, blocking a batsman's favourable scoring strokes with shrewd field placings. Illingworth later had a spell as chairman of selectors.

Mike Brearley Captained England in 31 Tests, losing only four of them. The Middlesex batsman's natural flair for dealing with people saw him pursue a career as a psychoanalyst after retiring from cricket.

Richie Benaud A charismatic captain who helped Australia regain the Ashes in 1958–59. The crafty leg-spinner then guided the Aussies to two successful defences of the Ashes. He became the first Test player to complete the double of 200 wickets and 2,000 runs.

Ian Chappell An effective rather than graceful batsman, Chappell captained Australia in 30 Tests, winning fifteen and losing just five. He had strong self-belief and believed that team goals were paramount, never losing a series during his time in charge.

Allan Border Not a natural leader, Border reluctantly took on the role of Australia's captain at a low point in their history. But he led them to a World Cup win in 1987 and they regained the Ashes two years later. Border captained his country a record 93 times and finished his career with a batting average of 50.

Sir Garfield Sobers Viewed by many as the finest all-rounder in the modern game, Sobers was an enterprising captain who led the West Indies in 39 Tests. In 1960, he made a then-record Test innings of 365 not out against Pakistan. He also became the first player to hit six sixes in one over when playing for Nottinghamshire against Glamorgan in 1968.

Clive Lloyd Captained the legendary West Indies side of the 1970s and 1980s. Under his leadership, the West Indies enjoyed a run of 26 Tests without defeat which included eleven successive wins. Lloyd was a hard-hitting middle-order batsman who also excelled in the field.

Imran Khan A dashing all-rounder who took 362 Test wickets for Pakistan and scored nearly 4,000 runs. He captained his country on 48 occasions and led them to victory in the 1992 World Cup.

Thrashings

A devastating bowling performance, or a destructive innings with the bat can help to inspire teammates and demoralise the opposition, sometimes to the extent that only three innings are required, as the beaten side fail at both attempts to reach the target. Here we take a closer look at some of the spankings that fall into this category.

1. England v Australia, 1938 – England won by an innings and 579 runs
Len Hutton opened the innings with a breathtaking 364, assisted by

Maurice Leyland's 187 and 'Young Joe' Hardstaff's 169 not out, England progressed to 903 for 7 declared. The Australian batting line-up was decimated by injuries to Don Bradman and Jack Fingleton and, at a packed Oval, the tourists fell to 201 and 123 all out.

2. South Africa v Australia, 2001-02 – Australia won by an innings and 360 runs

Damien Martyn and Adam Gilchrist's sixth wicket partnership of 317 laid the foundations for this crushing victory, with Australia's wicket-keeper finishing on 204 not out in a total of 652 for 7 declared. South Africa's reply of 159 did nothing to alleviate the pressure from Australia, and, in the follow-on, Glenn McGrath collected figures of 5 for 21, as the Proteas were skittled out for 133.

3. India v West Indies, 1958-59 – West Indies won by an innings and 336 runs

Rohan Kanhai's 256, including 42 fours, was ably supported by Basil Butcher (103), and Gary Sobers (106 not out). The West Indies score of 614 for 5 declared set the scene for Roy 'Gilly' Gilchrist's finest hour, as the hostile Jamaican generated tremendous pace from the Eden Park pitch to claim match figures of 9 for 73, with India falling to 124 and 154.

4. Australia v England, 1946-47 – Australia won by an innings and 332 runs

The Australians ripped through Wally Hammond's team at the first Test in Brisbane. Bradman weighed in with a majestic 187 and Lindsay Hassett hit 128 in a first innings total of 645. But Keith Miller made the biggest contribution with a knock of 79 and match figures of 9 for 77, as England posted scores of 141 and 172.

5. Pakistan v New Zealand, 2001-02 – Pakistan won by an innings and 324 runs

Inzaman-ul-Haq hit 329, clubbing a mighty 47 boundaries, including nine sixes, as Pakistan made 643. New Zealand's innings were no less dramatic as Shoaib Akhtar's spell of 6 for 11 saw the Kiwis' collapse to 73 all out. However, the chastened tourists managed to recover some pride second time around as Stephen Fleming's 66 helped them to 246 all out.

6. New Zealand v West Indies, 1994–95 – West Indies won by an innings and 322 runs

Stuart Williams may well feel as bad as the New Zealanders about this match, as he was only the West Indies player who failed to score at least 50 at the crease. Their first innings total of 660 for 5 comprised three hundreds and three fifties, Jimmy Adams scoring highest with 151. Williams didn't get a second bite at the apple as New Zealand fell for 216 and 122, with Courtney Walsh putting on a bowling masterclass to finish with match figures of 13 for 55.

7. Bangladesh v West Indies, 2002–03 – West Indies won by an innings and 310 runs

When Bangladesh opened the match with 139 all out in Dhaka, the West Indies weren't particularly scared. Nor were they intimidated by the Test minnows' bowling attack, as they amassed 536 all out. Needing 397 to make the visitors bat again, too many of the host batsmen 'ducked' their responsibility, as a Test record six batsmen failed to trouble the scorers. Jermaine Lawson claimed the exceptional figures of 6 for 3.

8. England v India, 1974 – England won by an innings and 285 runs
England were far from hospitable at the home of cricket, as Chris
Old tore through India at Lord's. Old's second innings return of 5
for 21 gave him nine wickets for the match, as he and Geoff
Arnold bowled out the Indians for 42. The tourists had fared
better in their previous attempt, answering England's imposing
629 with a score of 302.

9. Pakistan v Bangladesh, 2001–02 – Pakistan won by an innings
and 264 runs
Danish Kaneria outshone his more celebrated bowling partners
Wasim Akram and Waqar Younis with figures of 6 for 42, and 6
for 52. Bangladesh got things started with 134, but were then
made to toil in the field as Pakistan racked up 546 for 3 declared.
Faisal Iqbal, with nine, was the only batsman of the six not to
reach three figures as Inzamam retired hurt. Bangladesh improved,
in their second innings to 148 all out.

10. South Africa v Australia, 1949-50 - Australia won by an innings
and 259 runs
Arthur Morris, Neil Harvey and skipper Lindsay Hassett all scored
centuries as Australia posted a first innings total of 549 for 7
declared. South Africa struggled to muster much of a response, as
Keith Miller's 4 for 42 restricted the home side to a score of 158,
which they followed with 132 to confirm defeat.

Chases – Biggest Successful run chases in Tests

DATE	MATCH	GROUND	CHASE	SCORE
2002–2003	WI v Aus	Antigua	418	418/7
1948	ENG v Aus	Headingley	404	404/3
1975–1976	WI v Ind	Queen's Park	403	406/4
1999–2000	AUS v Pak	Bellerive Oval	369	369/6
1977–1978	WI v Aus	Bourda	359	362/7
1968–1969	NZ v WI	Eden Park	345	348/5
1984	ENG v WI	Lord's	342	344/1
1977–1978	AUS v Ind	WACA	339	342/8
1949–1950	SA v Aus	Kingsmead	336	336/5
2001–2002	SA v Aus	Kingsmead	335	340/5

1. West Indies

At Antigua in May 2003, the West Indies rescued some pride after comprehensively losing the first three games of a four-game series against Australia. With both sides all out for 240 in their first innings, the tourists took command with a first-wicket partnership of 242, and a total of 417. The West Indies were not to be beaten, however, and Ramnaresh Sarwan, and Shivnarine Chanderpaul both scored centuries on the way to a record successful run chase of 418.

2. Australia

The first side to score 400 runs in the final innings and win a Test match, Australia's record chase at Headlingley in 1948 stood for nearly 55 years. The tourists, chasing 404, were led to an improbable victory by Arthur Morris (182), and Don Bradman

(173*), who put on a spectacular second-wicket partnership of 301, as Australia won by seven wickets, finishing with 404 for 3.

3. India

Having built up a lead of 402 over India at Port of Spain in April 1976, the West Indies declared at 271 for 6 in their second innings. The tourists were not dismayed by their target, though, and, with Sunil Gavaskar hitting 102 and Gundappa Viswanath's 112, the total was reached with six wickets remaining as they scored 406 for 4.

4. Australia

The Australians never know when they're beaten and, after Shane Warne took 5 for 110 to end the Pakistan innings, they needed 369 to win the match. Knowing they needed the highest score to win a Test in Australia, they rushed to 369 for 6, with Justin Langer making 127, and Adam Gilchrist 149 off 163 balls, hitting 238 for the sixth wicket, at Hobart, in 1999.

5. Australia

At Georgetown in 1978 the West Indies took control of the third Test with a second innings score of 439. With Australia falling to 22 for 3, the target of 359 seemed very distant, but Graeme 'the Kamikaze Kid' Wood (126) and Craig Serjeant (124) putting on 251 for the fourth wicket, the tourists got to 362 for 7 to win the Test.

6. West Indies

New Zealand put on a fine batting display at Auckland leaving the visitors needing 345 for victory. But the West Indies refused to buckle under the pressure and Seymour Nurse added 168 to his first innings 95 to record a win with five wickets to spare.

7. West Indies

England declared on 300–9 in their second innings at Lord's leaving the West Indies requiring 342 to win, with time against them. Hoping Ian Botham might reproduce some of his first innings magic, when he took 8 for 103, England were bitterly disappointed as Gordon Greenidge made 214 off 242 balls, and guided the land of his birth to victory over the land of his childhood by nine wickets, scoring 344 off just 66.1 overs.

8. Australia

Coming in at 13 for 1 chasing a score of 339, Tony Mann was the night-watchman against India in Perth in 1977. Falling to 33 for 2 before stumps on day four, Mann was inspirational on the final day, as he hit an electrifying 105, in only his second Test, helping to win a thrilling game by two wickets.

9. Australia

A thrilling match at Durban was decided by Neil Harvey's 151 not out, as Australia reached their target of 336 for the loss of five wickets. It was a marked improvement on their first innings total of 75, in the third Test of 1949–50.

10. South Africa

South Africa got their revenge on Australia at Durban half a century later, as Herschelle Gibbs masterminded the host's successful chase with his 104. The Proteas won by five wickets as they went after the Baggy Green's total of 335.

* = Not Out

Fantasy XIs

Most teams in any sport will have one or two players who are outstanding in each generation. Sometimes, you may be lucky enough to see a team where each player is the best in his or her position, but it's rare. It's a subject open to much debate, but what if you were able to bring together the best players ever to have graced a pitch for their country . . . well, a cricket fan can dream

Asian Fantasy XI

Sunil Gavaskar (India)

The Indian's whopping total of 10,122 runs in 125 Tests puts him third highest on the all-time list, and he has scored more centuries – 34 – than any other batsman. He remains the only batsman to score three hundreds in a single Test.

Sachin Tendulkar (India)

Since his Test debut for India as a sixteen-year-old, the Little Master seemed destined for greatness. He averages over 56 runs, and has knocked a massive 33 centuries in 118 Tests – the first just a year after his debut. He made captain at 23.

Javed Miandad (Pakistan)

Hung up his bat in 1993 after a seventeen-year career with an average of 52.57 and a high score of 280 not out. Still Pakistan's highest run scorer with 8,832, almost 3,000 clear of his closest rival. In 34 Tests as captain he led his team to victory fourteen times, and lost only six.

Imran Khan (captain, Pakistan)

A great all-rounder and a shoe-in as captain. Proof? His batting average shot up from 25.43 to 52.34 when he was handed the skipper's mantle. Took 362 wickets in 88 Tests for Pakistan. Off the pitch he proved to be a proper ladies' man.

Kapil Dev (India)

Along with Ian Botham and Imran Khan, Kapil Dev is widely regarded as cricket's most complete all-rounder. He took 434 wickets in a 131-Test career for India and hit eight hundreds at an average 31.05.

Kumar Sangakkara (wicket-keeper, Sri Lanka)

The Oscar-Wilde-loving Sri Lankan keeper could almost make it onto this list as a specialist batsman. In his 44 matches he boasts an average of 49.78, and has hit 7 hundreds and 2 double centuries.

Aravinda De Silva (Sri Lanka)

The Sri Lankan's swashbuckling style is suited to the One-Day game, but in his eighteen-year Test career his average was consistently around the 40-mark.

Survived Sri Lanka's early days of Test status, scored 267 against the Kiwis in 1991, and can even bowl off-spin, which is usually brought out for the 50-over version of the game.

Wasim Akram (Pakistan)
An archetypal sting in the tail. How many lower-order batsmen can boast a high score of 257 not out? And that's before you factor in the 41 wickets he took at a miserly average of 23.62.

Bishan Singh Bedi (India)
Brilliant slow left-armer, who was no stranger to a bit of rabble-rousing. Led a faction calling for better pay during India's 1974 tour of England, and declared their innings over against the West Indies in protest at the hosts' intimidating bowling. He took 266 wickets at an average of 28.71.

Muttiah Muralitharan (Sri Lanka)
Trades places regularly with Shane Warne at the top of the wicket-taker tree. The Sri Lankan has breezed past the 500 mark with no sign of stopping. Temporarily hampered when his trademark doosra was outlawed, he has taken nine wickets in an innings twice in his career – once for just 51 runs.

Waqar Younis (Pakistan)
The Pakistani paceman's fast in-swingers were so dangerous that he made Martin Crowe wear a face guard for the first time in his career. He took 55 wickets in his first eleven Tests, including

5 five-wicket hauls and had taken 373 wickets – almost 60 per cent clean bowled or lbw – at an average of 23.56 by the time he retired.

Australia Fantasy XI

Bill Lawry
Brilliant, if dour, opener who averaged 47.15 in 67 Tests. One of the first players to break the unwritten rule of walking, he was singled out as a key reason for the decline in gentlemanly standards in the game. Became the first Australian captain to be sacked in the middle of a series when he lost the job to Ian Chappell.

Mark Taylor
Over 100 Tests, nineteen centuries and a top score of 334 – ENOUGH SAID. Bowlers considered themselves lucky if they got this marathon merchant out before he hit 50.

Matthew Hayden
With an average of 55.46 Hayden would be a nightmare prospect for opening bowlers from any era. Scored a mammoth 380 in 2003, albeit against Zimbabwe.

Donald Bradman
The Don. The feats he attained in his twenty-year career are unlikely to be matched – ever. He averaged 99.94 and still holds the Aussie record for second-, fourth-, fifth- AND sixth-wicket stands. Little known Don fact: he bagged two wickets as a spin bowler, against the West Indies and England, both times at the Adelaide Oval.

Steve Waugh (captain)

As captain he oversaw Australia's most successful period before retiring after 168 Tests with 10,927 runs. He won an incredible 41 of the 50 Tests he was in charge of, after revolutionising the tactics of the five-day game. When he hung up his baggy green cap he was the second highest Test scorer and the second greatest century maker with 32 centuries.

Ian Healy (wicket-keeper)

A batsman's nightmare, at 395 scalps, he has dismissed more than any other keeper. And with four centuries and a top score of 161 not out, he has proved he is no slouch with the bat.

Ritchie Benaud

Now known as the smooth voice of cricket to fans around the world, he was once one of Australia's best captains. His leg breaks and googlies sent batsmen into knots, but he credits his successes as captain as being the result of learning to bat. And he did all right, averaging 24.45 over 63 matches.

Shane Warne

The flipper expert's legendary status was tainted in 2003 following an ill-judged decision to lose weight by taking a banned diuretic. Now firmly on the straight and narrow, he regularly swaps top wicket-taker spot with Muttiah Muralitharan with over 500 scalps.

Craig McDermott

Raw power summed up this player's game. He was part of the all-conquering Aussie side of the late 80s and early 90s, and took 291 wickets, at an average of 28.63, over 71 matches.

FANTASY XIs

Dennis Lillee

The Menace was the scourge of batsmen everywhere, but he took special relish in dismissing Englishmen. His overall average was 23.92 but against the Poms it was 21.00. He finally bagged 355 wickets. If it wasn't for a back injury, which kept him out of action for two years, we can only guess how many more he would have taken.

Glenn McGrath

Believe it or not, this sledging expert from the NSW countryside was told by his captain at Narromine he had no future as a bowler. At an average of just over 21 runs per wicket, he is edging ever closer to the 500-scalp mark. He scored his maiden Test half century in 2004, eleven years after his debut.

England Fantasy XI

The selectors usually get it in the neck whomever they pick for a Test side, so here is a team guaranteed to get an argument going. Based on a mixture of statistics, character and big-match temperament, this is an England XI to match any other. They might even have won the odd match.

Geoffrey Boycott

The dogged Yorkshireman racked up more than 100 centuries in his career and is the only England player to bat on all days of a five-day Test (v Australia at Trent Bridge, 1977).

Jack Hobbs
Known as 'The Master', Hobbs was cricket's most prolific batsman, scoring over 61,000 first-class runs. The Surrey and England legend became the first cricketer to be knighted, in 1953.

David Gower
The classy left-hander could stroke a drive through the covers and make the bowler happy just to have been at the ground to watch it. He played more than 100 Tests for England, but should have played many more.

Len Hutton
Recognised as one of the greatest batsmen the game has ever produced, the Yorkshire player became England's first professional captain and he proved to be a fine leader in 1952, against India.

Colin Cowdrey
The Kent batsman was the first man to play 100 Tests and also the first English cricketer to be given a peerage when he became Lord Cowdrey of Tonbridge in 1997.

Denis Compton
An exuberant character, who was not afraid to take risks with his bat, the Middlesex star was a loose-limbed batsman who could play all the strokes.

Ian Botham
An inspirational all-rounder, who made headlines on and off the field, his legendary performance in the 1981 Ashes against Australia was one of the great British sporting moments.

FANTASY XIs

Alan Knott

The Kent and England wicket-keeper hardly missed a chance behind the stumps. He was also a more than useful batsman, compiling five Test centuries.

Derek Underwood

The Kent left-arm spinner was nicknamed 'Deadly' for the havoc he caused on rain-hit pitches. He took nearly 300 wickets for England and would have had more, if he had not joined the rebel tour of South Africa in 1981–82.

Fred Trueman

Yorkshire's 'Fiery Fred' was the first player from any country to take 300 Test wickets. He boasted a classical easy action and had a great control of swing.

Jim Laker

The Surrey and England spinner earned his place in the record books at Old Trafford in 1956 when he took nineteen Australian wickets for 90 runs. A unique feat in a first-class match which may never be repeated.

New Zealand Fantasy XI

New Zealand is not the biggest or most successful country in the world, but it has a proud cricketing history. Our resident Kiwi expert has selected this side as the all-time New Zealand Fantasy XI as being good enough to take on and beat all comers.

John Wright

Scored 5,334 runs in a fifteen-year career at an average of 37.83. Opened the batting in all but four of his 148 innings, and is still the NZ record holder for a second-wicket partnership. Currently India coach.

Bruce Edgar

Played just 39 matches in his eighteen-year career from 1978 to 1986, but made his mark in every innings he appeared in. Opened in all but three of his Test innings, and hit twelve half centuries and three 100s.

Martin Crowe

On the outside, it looked as if the profusely-sweating former captain felt the heat on a daily basis, but he was cool under the surface. Best remembered for his 299 against Sri Lanka – a New Zealand record – at the Basin Reserve. Also a useful medium-pace bowler. Cousin of film star Russell Crowe.

Stephen Fleming (captain)

The tactical genius is widely regarded as the best captain in world cricket. Assumed skippering duties three years after making his Test debut in 1994. Scored a massive 274 not out against Sri Lanka.

Nathan Astle

Holder of the record for the fastest double century, with his 222 not out against England. Could be opener if Wright or Edgar fail fitness tests.

FANTASY XIs

Ian Smith (wicket-keeper)
Now known for his friendly Kiwi drawl offsetting Ritchie Benaud's encyclopaedic commentary on Tests, the short-necked keeper was once one of the best in the game. Made 168 catches in 63 matches, and was also handy with the bat, and scored a couple of centuries. Even bowled once – three overs against the West Indies in 1985.

Chris Cairns
Known as 'Lance's son' when he burst on the scene in 1989, but his all-round performances soon eclipsed his Excalibur-wielding dad. His best match haul was against the West Indies in 1999, when he took 10 wickets for 100. Despite a career blighted by injury, he still boasts a batting average of over 33.

Sir Richard Hadlee
His 431 Test wickets were once a world record, and he is still known as one of the best quick bowlers on the planet. And he could bat a bit as well: he holds the sixth wicket partnership record of 246 with Jeff Crowe, and scored 15 fifties and two centuries in a career lasting from 1973 to 1990.

John Bracewell
The current Kiwi coach ended his playing career on a remarkably symmetrical 1001 runs – in which his best score was 110. The off-spinner took 102 wickets in a ten-year career

Daniel Vettori
Spectacled Vettori became the youngest Test bowler in NZ cricket history when he arrived on the scene as an eighteen-year-

old. His first scalp was former England captain Nasser Hussain, and he became the youngest player to take 100 wickets. Back problems affected his bowling, but he has since become a useful lower-order batsman, and made 137 not out batting at number nine against Pakistan in 2003.

Ewen Chatfield
Chats continually bowled in the shadow of Hadlee, but proved to be a useful foil, taking 123 wickets at an average of 32.18. His batting stats scream 'number 11' – in 43 Tests, he could only muster a top score of 21 not out, at an average of 8.57.

South Africa Fantasy XI

South Africa have had their fair share of ups and downs on the pitch, but they have also produced some true cricketing gems.

Herschelle Gibbs
The opening batsman epitomises the new South Africa after apartheid. Dashing and full of flare with strokes all round the wicket, Gibbs has shown tremendous character to come back from his brush with the law in the 'match-fixing' scandal to rack up nearly 5,000 runs so far.

Barry Richards
Even though he only played four Tests for South Africa before they were banned from international sport, Richards was in a class apart when it came to batting. Often accused of getting bored because the game was simply too easy for him, he played with

great distinction for Hampshire and, together with Gordon Greenidge, terrified opening bowling attacks.

Gary Kirsten

The recently retired left-hander played 101 Test matches and at times single-handedly carried his team to totals they had no right in getting. Some call him dour and boring, but they are being unkind. He had the shots, but he knew when to use them. A genuine nugget of a player.

Jacques Kallis

Simply the most gifted South African cricketer to play for the rainbow nation since their return to the international game. He averages nearly 55 with the bat and scored centuries in four consecutive matches in 2004. Not a bad bowler too with over 150 Test wickets.

Graeme Pollock

Voted South Africa's cricketer of the century in 2000, Graeme Pollock was a left-handed batting geninus. He too had his career cut short by international sanctions, but gave the world enough of a glimpse of his talent to leave no one in any doubt of his class, leaving the game with an average second only to Don Bradman.

Kepler Wessels

Kepler Wessels had the great honour of leading the team back from international exile in 1992 and carried out the role with distinction. He led the Proteas to victory in their first Test match back at Lord's and was a more than useful middle-order batsman. He also played for Australia during South Africa's ban.

Eddie Barlow

The bespectacled all-rounder was a talented batsman, who could have done so much more had he been given the chance. Still, he managed to score over 2,500 runs in his 30 matches and was part of the South African team that out-classed everyone during the 60s. Nicknamed 'Billy Bunter' Barlow was a much loved character who played the game in the best spirit.

Mark Boucher

Boucher took over the gloves from Dave Richardson as an eager twenty-year-old, but he quickly made the spot his own claiming record after record along the way. He is the most successful wicket-keeper in South African history having reached the double of 1,000 runs and 100 dismissals. He was the fastest in the world to make 100 ODI catches (in his 65th match) and the quickest to claim 150 Test dismissals (38 Tests), and is a capable captain whenever called upon.

Shaun Pollock

Keeping up the family name can be hard, but Shaun Pollock has done it and then some. Opening the bowling with Allan Donald, he helped create one of the most formidable attacks in world cricket with a line and length that seemed mechanical in its accuracy. He can bat, too, having scored two Test-match centuries.

Allan Donald

'White Lightning' was a terrifying prospect for most batsmen to face and rightly so. Donald was the first South African to take more than 300 Test wickets and did so with a speed verging on the life threatening. His famous duel with Mike Atherton in 1998 is the stuff of legend and was Test cricket at its most intense. Batsmen can sleep a little easier now.

Mike Proctor

The burly fast bowler formed a deadly partnership with Peter Pollock during the 60s and even though he played only seven Tests, Richie Benaud reckons he could have walked into any team after the war. He played for Gloucestershire and had an enormous impact to the point where the team were often referred to as Proctorshire.

West Indies Fantasy XI

The West Indies will always be loved for their cricket around the world because they didn't just win games, they won them with a panache unique to the Caribbean. This XI would give many an opposition a sleepless night.

Gordon Greenidge

Formed one half of one of the most devastating opening partnerships in world cricket with Desmond Haynes. His attacking style put teams on the back foot from the off, and an average of 44.72 is incredible for an opening batsman.

Desmond Haynes

Also remarkably, averaged over forty as an opening batsman and put on sixteen century stands with Greenidge, with four of those passing the 200 mark. His retirement in 1994 signalled the end of an era for West Indies cricket.

Brian Lara

The left-hander has over 10,000 Test runs – all the more impressive because he has performed in an era where West Indies cricket is in decline. He has twice broken the world record for the highest test score and is the current holder with his amazing 400 not out against England in March 2004.

George Headley

The first great West Indies batsman, Headley's prowess led many to proclaim him the 'black Bradman' and Bradman the 'white Headley'! In just 22 Tests, Headley scored 2,190 runs with an average of 60.83.

Sir Viv Richards

Bowlers around the world breathed a sigh of relief when Richards retired in 1991. Averaging over 50 with 24 hundreds to his name, he captained his side to 27 test wins.

Sir Gary Sobers

Proclaimed by many in the game as the greatest all-rounder of all time after scoring over 8,000 test runs and taking 235 wickets with the ball, Gary Sobers was the first batsman to hit 6 sixes in an over off Glamorgan's Malcolm Nash while playing for Nottinghamshire in 1968.

Jeffrey Dujon

In a Test career spanning ten years, Dujon's hands took a regular beating from the West Indies quicks. But he was up to the challenge, taking 265 catches as well as averaging nearly 32 with the bat.

Malcolm Marshall

He was one of the shortest of the West Indies quicks, but arguably the most deadly in his prime. Marshall's ability to swing the ball at great pace helped him take 376 wickets at an impressive strike rate of 46.7.

Michael Holding

Known as a quiet friendly man off the square, Holding was quite the opposite with a ball in his hand. He bowled with frightening pace and holds the best Test figures for a West Indies bowler with 14 for 149 against England in 1976.

Curtly Ambrose

He is the second highest wicket-taking bowler in West Indies history with 405, and a tormentor of England in particular – Ambrose's 6 for 24 infamously helped bowl England out for just 46 in 1994. His figures of 7 for 1 against the Australians the year before clinched a series win in amazing fashion.

Courtney Walsh

Emerged out of the shadow of Ambrose and Marshall to become the first bowler in the world to take 500 test wickets and established himself as one of the game's greats.

In Your Dreams!

Left-handed Fantasy XI

Only ten per cent of the world is left-handed and as a result much of their lives are spent trying to get ahead in a right-handed world. It can be hard for much of the time, but put a cricket bat or a ball into their hands and life can often become ridiculously easy. Below are some of the left-handed cricketers who have excelled and excited fans with their interpretation of a game for everybody.

John Edrich
Edrich was a stocky, opening batsmen who showed an enormous amount of courage whenever he played, especially when facing some of the most hostile bowlers in the world. He was knocked out cold by a ball from South Africa's Peter Pollock and had his ribs broken by a Dennis Lillee thunderbolt. But it didn't stop him playing 77 Tests for England and scoring over 5,000 runs.

Mark Taylor
Taylor took over the reigns as Australia captain from Allan Border

and proceeded to turn an up-and-coming team into world beaters. He was a doughty cricketer, who never let his team down and memorably, when his back was against the wall on the 1997 Ashes tour, produced a match-winning century to silence his critics before going on to equal Don Bradman's record Test score of 334 not out.

David Gower

Probably the most elegant left-hander of them all. The dashing Gower could produce innings of such beauty that cricket often ceased to be a sport and became an art form when he was at the wicket. He endured some testing times as captain of England and perhaps should never have taken the role. Instead, he should have focused on the finer things in life like the extra cover drive.

Clive Lloyd

Lloyd will forever be remembered as the man who led the West Indies through their most successful sporting era of all time, using the talents of his fast bowlers to maximum advantage. But to forget about his own abilities would be a travesty. Lloyd played over 100 Tests, scoring more than 7,500 runs and could strike a ball as hard as Viv Richards or field a ball as quickly as Jonty Rhodes. A great player.

Alvin Kallicharan

Kallicharan was a wristy left-hander with all the strokes in the book. In playing 66 Tests for the West Indies in the 70s and 80s, he was part of an incredible side that took the world by storm and he made a very real contribution. Centuries against an Australia side that had Lillee and Thompson steaming in at their best were a highlight. Controversy followed him later in his career when he went to play in South Africa during apartheid.

Larry Gomes
One of the most stylish cricketers ever to have come out of the West Indies and that says a lot. He struggled to impose himself on a team full of all-time greats, but the fact that he eventually did was a testament to his character as well as his ability. Several times he dug his team out of a hole when the supposed better batsmen had failed.

Adam Gilchrist
Apparently Gilchrist is a wicket-keeper and a fine one at that. But incredibly he is a man that would stroll into any Test team in the world as one of their frontline batsmen. Gilchrist embodies Australia's dominance of world cricket, scoring his runs faster than most One-Day players and he does it with alarming regularity. An average of over 50 from his 60-plus Tests is quite astonishing.

Chaminda Vaas
Whenever Sri Lanka play cricket all eyes are on Muttiah Muralitharan. But if all credit to Sri Lanka's bowling performances were given to Murali too, there might well be rioting in the streets of Colombo. Vaas is a dedicated cricketer who toils away on spinner-friendly pitches on the sub-continent and still manages to take plenty of wickets. He has sublime control of the ball and will soon reach 300 Test wickets – richly deserved.

Derek Underwood
Deadly Derek was a left-arm spinner of pure class. He played 86

Tests for England during the successes of the 60s and 70s and was always a handful regardless of the wickets they played on. He left the international scene just three wickets shy of the magical 300 mark, but his contribution was felt throughout the team.

Alf Valentine

One half of 'those two little friends of mine – Sonny Ramadhin and Alf Valentine', the left-arm spinner had a big presence and spun the ball prodigiously. He might only have played two first-class games before the West Indies tour to England in 1950 but he made the most of his chance before going on to play 36 times for the Caribbean. He died in May 2004

Alan Davidson

Davidson was a classic Australian left-arm seam bowler with unbelievable control. His finest hour was the tied Test of 1960 against the West Indies, which he went into with a broken finger and came out of with a significant record – the first man to score 100 runs and take ten wickets in a Test. He was a captain's dream, offering penetration with a miserly average (under 21).

The Tallest XI

The following lofty cricketers could have made a living playing basketball. As it was, they were all tall, but brilliant, cricketers. They are the *Amazing Cricket Facts*' Tallest XI.

Will Jefferson

At a towering 6 ft 10 in, the Essex opener is usually the first to know when it starts to rain.

Adrian Rollins
The tall former Derbyshire and Northants opener used his height (6 ft 5 in) to good effect.

Tom Moody
The 6 ft 6 in Aussie was a big-hitting batsman and medium-pace swing bowler.

Clive Lloyd
The 6 ft 5 in captain of an all-conquering West Indies side, Lloyd's stooped figure, carrying a heavy bat, was a familiar sight to all fans of the game.

Jacob Oram
The 6 ft 7in all-rounder is believed to be the tallest player ever to play for New Zealand.

Tony Greig
A commanding figure at 6 ft 7in, Greig has a place in the record books as the tallest player to represent England.

Ray Jennings
At 6 ft 1 in, the South African was tall for a wicket-keeper, flying with ease to third slip to take catches.

Chris Tremlett
The Hampshire bowler's 6 ft 7in frame made long car journeys difficult, creating a disc problem, until he had corrective surgery and found a vehicle with sufficient head room.

IN YOUR DREAMS!

Dean Headley
The 6 ft 5in fast bowler found plenty of movement off the s
eam and looked set for a long Test career with England.
But a persistent back injury brought about his premature
retirement.

Glenn McGrath
The 6ft 6in giant has been a mainstay of the Australian attack,
taking over 400 Test wickets.

Joel Garner
The West Indies fast bowler, standing 6 ft 8in tall, was once asked
by an enquiring female if everything was 'in proportion'. 'Lady,' he
replied, 'if it was, I would be eight foot six!'

The Smallest XI

If these players had failed to make the grade in cricket, they could
have considered becoming jockeys…

Sunil Gavaskar
The legendary Indian opener stands at just 5 ft 5in, but he made
many big scores in his illustrious career.

Bobby Abel
The one-time Surrey and England batsman had a tiny 5 ft 4 in
frame. There was no truth in the rumour that he also worked as a
lumberjack on a mushroom farm.

Harry Pilling
At just 5 ft 3 in, the former Lancashire batsman would struggle to get on some of the rides at Alton Towers.

Sir Don Bradman
Although only 5 ft 7 in tall, the legendary Aussie was a giant in cricketing terms, viewed by many as the greatest batsman of all time.

Sachin Tendulkar
Another batsman who has not let his lack of inches hold him back. The 5 ft 4 in Indian continues to command bowling attacks.

Tatenda Taibu
The Zimbabwe wicket-keeper is the youngest ever captain in Test history and probably the shortest, standing at 5 ft 4 in.

Tony Cottey
Most people look down on the former Sussex and Glamorgan star. The Welshman is a tiny 5 ft 4 in.

Johnny Briggs
Not to be confused with the actor who plays *Coronation Street*'s Mike Baldwin, the diminutive slow bowler (5 ft 5 in) played for Lancashire and England around the turn of the nineteenth century.

Alfred Freeman
Known as 'Tich', the 5 ft 2 in former Kent and England player is recognised as one of the finest slow bowlers the game has ever known.

IN YOUR DREAMS!

Khaled Mahmud
The Bangladesh medium pacer, at only slightly over five feet in height, could legitimately make a claim to being the shortest bowler in One-Day international history.

Ramakant Desai
The Indian fast bowler measured just 5 ft 4 in. His imaginative teammates nicknamed him 'Tiny'.

Fattest XI

Sportsmen are usually fit, toned specimens, who spend hours working out in the gym. But there are of course some notable exceptions in cricket! That said, this team would still take some eating. Or should that be beating?

David Boon
The moustachioed Aussie batsman was a legendary drinker who allegedly consumed 56 cans of lager during the flight to England for the 1989 Ashes series.

Mike Gatting
The ex-Middlesex and England skipper didn't mind being called anything, as long as it wasn't late for lunch.

Colin Milburn
Nicknamed 'Ollie' after the equally rotund comedy actor Oliver Hardy, the 18-stone Durham lad was a real character who enjoyed a drink.

Greg Ritchie
The portly batsman's physique counted against him when the Australian selectors decided in the mid-1980s that litheness in the field was an important requirement.

Robert Key
The Kent and England batsman was told to slim down after seeing his weight balloon to 16 stones.

Inzamam-ul-Haq
Known as 'The Potato', the Pakistan ace is said to loathe exercise and regularly sits back in a wicker chair while the rest of his team get put through their fielding drills.

Eddie Barlow
The chunky South African's untidy appearance led to commentator Charles Fortune saying he was running in to bowl 'looking like an unmade bed'.

Andrew Flintoff
After being upset by comments in the press about his ample frame, Flintoff commented that it was 'not bad for a fat lad' after picking up a Man of the Match award for England.

David Bairstow
The one-time Yorkshire and England wicket-keeper was surprisingly agile despite his bulky frame.

Eddie Hemmings
The ex-Nottinghamshire and England spinner was known as 'The Whale' and it is fair to say he had a healthy appetite.

IN YOUR DREAMS!

Ian Austin
The former Lancashire and England cut an unlikely sporting figure with a waistline said to be 'somewhere between Billy Bunter and Friar Tuck'.

Merv Hughes
The larger-than-life Aussie paceman gave everything on the field, then often tried to drink everything off it. A genuine competitor who played hard, drank harder and soaked it all up with the odd pie or few.

No Ball

Funny Old Name

There's enough pressure on professional cricketers without the whole crowd laughing at them when they are announced to the crowd, but that's just an extra problem some men have to deal with...

Julien Wiener
The big Victorian opened the batting for his state and country at the end of the 70s and start of the 80s.

John Crapp
A sound left-handed batsman for Gloucestershire for twenty years, the Cornishman also played for England.

Richard Daft
Second only to W G Grace in the national batting averages on four occasions, the Nottinghamshire batsman wasn't as silly as his name suggests.

NO BALL

Julius Caesar
With such a grand name to live up to, life was always going to be tough, but Caesar enjoyed eighteen years playing for Surrey and Lancashire in the mid-nineteenth century.

Rana saheb Shri Sir Natwarsinghji Bhavsinghji, the Maharaja of Porbandar
Captain of the Indian team touring England in 1932, the Maharajah was ruler of a little state in what is now Gujarat.

Ted Badcock
A medium-pace bowler, and a handy batsman, Badcock played more than twenty years for Wellington and Otago, as well as representing New Zealand.

Sir Spencer Cecil Brabazon Ponsonby Fane
The treasurer for the MCC for 36 years, Ponsonby Fane was a lively batsman and wicket-keeper for Surrey and Middlesex.

Xenophon Balaskas
'Saxophone' was a leg-spin bowler, and a useful tail-end batsman, who loved his cricket for South Africa, and many of the state sides in his home country.

Arif Butt
A fast-medium bowler, Arif Butt was part of the first Pakistan side to tour Australia.

Percy Hornibrook
A tall, left-arm bowler for Queensland and Australia, Hornibrook played his best cricket between the wars.

Geffery Noblet

With an amusing surname and a mis-spelled first name Noblet still enjoyed a good career bowling for South Australia and the Baggy Greens.

Relative Success

Being a successful professional sportsman is not an easy thing to achieve. The vast majority fail. But this lot have more than one success in the clan and they show that some families have cricket in the blood, producing two or more players!

Grace

The great W G Grace was a member of a remarkably gifted cricketing family. His brothers Edward and Fred also played for Gloucestershire and England. A third brother, Henry, appeared for Gloucestershire. W G's two sons also played the game. W G Junior turned out for Gloucestershire while Charles was with London County.

Foster

The Foster family produced seven brothers who played for Worcestershire. They were Basil, Henry, Maurice, Neville, Reginald, Geoffrey and Wilfrid.

Headley

Legendary West Indies batsman George Headley produced a son, Ron, who also represented his country, albeit with a lesser degree of success. Ron's son, Dean, also played Test cricket, but for the country of his birth, England.

NO BALL

Compton

The Compton brothers, Denis and Les, were together at Middlesex. They also played professional football in tandem for Arsenal. Batsman Denis was one of the all-time greats for England, but wicket-keeper Les failed to make the step up from the county side.

Chappell

A trio of Chappell brothers, Greg, Ian and Trevor, played Test cricket for Australia. Ian and Greg were leading players who both had spells as captain. Trevor, who made only three Test appearances, is best remembered for controversially bowling underarm to New Zealand's Brian McKechnie, under instruction from Greg.

Stewart

Alec Stewart enjoyed a much longer Test career than his father, Micky. Alec was capped 133 times, while Micky made just eight appearances for England. Father and son both gave loyal service to Surrey.

Greig

Brothers Tony and Ian Greig both played for England. Tony captained his country, but his significantly lesser-talented sibling made just two Test appearances.

Cowdrey

Colin Cowdrey and his sons Chris and Graham all played for Kent. Chris emulated his father by representing England. Graham remained with Kent until 1998, ensuring there was a Cowdrey on the county's books for a 48-year span.

Butcher
When Mark Butcher played his first game for Surrey against his father Alan's Glamorgan, it was the first time ever father and son faced each other in a match between first-class counties.

Crowe
Martin Crowe and his elder brother Jeff played for New Zealand. Martin made his first Test appearance at the age of just nineteen and went on to become a key player for his country while Jeff also made a useful contribution.

Waugh
Twins Steve and Mark Waugh played many Tests together for Australia. Mark was recognised as the one with more natural talent, but Steve's grit and determination made him a highly successful captain.

Hollioake
Ben Hollioake followed his elder brother Adam from the Surrey side to the England set-up. A naturally gifted all-round cricketer, Ben was tragically killed at the age of 24 in 2002, after crashing his car in Australia.

Bad Cricket Excuses

1. Bishen Singh Bedi
'Two days after the tour started the boys started counting the days when they would go back home,' 'Our phones were tapped,' 'They spied on us,' 'They were very hostile – the crowds, the

players, the press,' 'The atmosphere was not right. We didn't get turned on'. A series of ridiculous excuses for India's 1978 series defeat to Pakistan.

2. Sunil Gavaskar

'I didn't play 60 overs myself, that's obvious,' 'The awful noise made by the crowd didn't help my thinking'. Great excuses for a score of 36-not out in 60 overs against England.

3. England

England's worst ever Test score recorded in Johannesburg in 1999 was explained as the result of 'low cloud'.

4. Glenn McGrath

'No. 11 is probably the toughest place to bat. There are days when I'm hitting them well and the guy at the other end gets out. There must be a massive innings coming up to even everything all up.' That explains your career average of 7.27 then Glenn.

5. Hemang Badani

'Lee must have seen the white ball much more easily as it came out of your dark hand.' A brilliant excuse for Indian team-mate Lakshmipathy Balaji after Brett Lee won a VB series match at the SCG with a six from the penultimate ball of the innings.

6. Michael Vaughan

'Every time we snicked it, it went to hand. Every shot we played seemed to go down their throats; it was just not a good day to remember, really.' The England captain wasn't very happy with his first day in charge of the Test side.

7. Mark Richardson
'The South Africans really struggled to understand the principle of the whole thing. They're very competitive and they took it a bit seriously . . . because I lost, it goes down in the record book as an unofficial dead heat.' New Zealand slow coach and opening batsman Mark Richardson recalls his only recognised, by him anyway, defeat in his now traditional end-of-tour race against Neil McKenzie.

On The Head

This fine publication is the latest in a long line of books to have been written on the subject of cricket. Here is a selection of the popular titles that have also graced the sporting bookshelves:

In the Eye of the Typhoon: The Inside Story of the MCC Tour of Australia and New Zealand 1954–55 by Frank Tyson.
England's memorable win Down Under is covered by Tyson who kept a diary and took many photographs during the tour. The fast bowler's recollections of the tour are based on that diary, and illustrated with more than 100 photographs. An exceptionally written and visual history of one of the happiest and most successful tours in English cricket history.

Beyond A Boundary by C L R James
A blend of personal memoir, social history and sports commentary. James analyses the role cricket has played in his own life and in the history of the West Indies and England.

NO BALL

Opening Up by Geoff Boycott
The former Yorkshire and England opening batsman's autobiography reveals the secrets and the thinking behind his talents on the cricket pitch.

Another Bloody Tour by Frances Edmonds.
The controversial book was written after Frances accompanied her husband, spinner Phil Edmonds, on England's disastrous tour to the West Indies in 1986. She wrote another bestseller, *Cricket XXXX Cricket*, after covering the Ashes series in Australia in 1987.

Don't Tell Kath by Ian Botham with Peter Hayter.
The legendary all-rounder describes the triumphs, achievements and setbacks he has experienced in a remarkable career. A great collaboration by one of the game's greatest characters and one of its most respected journalists.

Dickie Bird: My Autobiography
The popular former Test umpire gives a behind-the-scenes account of the game and those involved in it.

Opening Up, My Autobiography by Mike Atherton
The former England captain gives a very personal account of his career in the game with some serious observations on English cricket and the world game today. Not such an original title, though.

Dazzler: The Autobiography by Darren Gough with David Norrie
Gough describes his cricketing adventures with Yorkshire and England. Subjects covered include an honest appraisal of England captains Atherton, Stewart and Hussain.

Shane Warne: My Autobiography
One of the most consistently newsworthy characters in sport
takes stock of a phenomenally successful career and also gives his
account of the accompanying scandals and controversies.

A Thirst For Life: With The Accent On Cricket by Henry Blofeld.
The cricket journalist and broadcaster's memoirs follow an elegant
journey from the playing fields of Eton in the 1950s to the muddy
waters of today's match fixing allegations.

Famous grounds

Many grounds around the world are used to stage Test cricket,
and some of them have become more famous in their own
right.

Lord's, home of Middlesex CCC, is renowned as the 'home of
cricket' and the game's spiritual 'headquarters'. The Long Room,
in the heart of the pavilion, features portraits of the game's best-
known figures, including the ground's founder, Thomas Lord.

The Oval, in Kennington, London, is the home of Surrey CCC.
The ground traditionally hosts the last Test match of each summer
in August, or September.

Trent Bridge in Nottingham is considered by players and
spectators to be one of the most pleasant cricket grounds in
England. The architecture has been kept within the parameters set
by the 1886 pavilion.

NO BALL

Melbourne Cricket Ground, Australia. Known as 'The People's Ground', it was built in 1853 and hosted the first-ever Test match. Once the latest building works have been completed, the ground will boast a seating capacity in excess of 100,000.

The WACA (Western Australian Cricket Association) Ground in Perth was officially opened in 1893. The Lillee-Marsh Stand at the ground was completed in 1988 and named after the former state and Australian international players Dennis Lillee and Rodney Marsh.

The Kensington Oval, in Bridgetown, Barbados, was the first West Indies ground to host an English touring team in 1895. The venue also hosted the first Test in the West Indies, against England, in 1930.

Sabina Park in Kingston, Jamaica, is one of the smallest but most picturesque grounds in the Caribbean. The highest ever Test score (849) was scored at the venue by England in 1930.

Eden Park in Auckland is recognised as New Zealand's major sports stadium. The venue saw New Zealand record the lowest ever Test score – 26 all out against England in 1955. Field settings are never easy due to the ground's diamond shape.

Gadaffi Stadium in Pakistan is now one of the most delightful grounds in world cricket, having had a facelift for the 1996 World Cup, when it hosted the Final. The ground's pitch is normally slow and helpful to spinners.

Eden Gardens in Calcutta is the oldest cricket ground in India and also considered to be one of the finest in the world. It has a maximum capacity of over 100,000, with crowds always averaging more than 50,000.

One Club Wonders

Not all sportsmen are in it for the money, some of them find a place where they enjoy themselves and are happy with their team-mates and coaches and stay there for their whole career. Although not so commonplace these days, there are still a few county legends in the mix.

Albert Alderman (Derbyshire)
Another county legend never to play for his country, Alderman was a dependable opening batsman who reached 1,000 runs in a season on six occasions. He scored 12,376 runs for Derbyshire from 1928–48, his only other club was Derby County as he also played professional football.

Jack Bannister (Warwickshire)
A right-arm, fast-medium bowler who took 100 wickets on four occasions during his nineteen seasons at Edgbaston, he claimed 1,198 wickets at 21.91, but was never selected for England. Jack went on to become secretary of the Cricketers' Association.

George Cox (Sussex)
George Rubens Cox served Sussex from 1895 until he retired in 1928. A left-arm bowler, whose flight and accuracy demanded

respect throughout his long career, he took 1,843 wickets at 22.86 and as a right-handed batsman worth a few runs, scored 14,643 at 18.77, he was never called upon to represent England.

George Cox (Sussex)

Upon his father's retirement Sussex were Cox-less for just three short years, as the younger Cox began his durable first-class career in 1931. He was a regular for 25 years, and played occasionally until 1961. A better batsman than his old man, he hit 22,949 runs at 32.93, including 50 centuries.

Harold Gibbons (Worcestershire)

'Doc' joined Worcestershire as a 22-year-old, from the Lord's ground staff in 1927. He played thirteen seasons at New Road until the outbreak of war in 1939, playing 380 matches, and played a further three matches in 1946. He holds the Worcestershire record for the most runs in a season with 2,654 in 1934, and is considered one of his county's finest batsmen not to play for England.

Canon Frank Gillingham (Essex)

The Reverend Canon Gillingham played in the days when there was no clash of interests on Sundays. He played as and when his ecclesiastical duties allowed for 25 years from 1903 to 1928, as a wicket-keeper and middle order batsman. He is the only Anglican clergyman to score a double-century at Lord's.

John Langridge (Sussex)

Another man who found 'Sussex by the sea' the place for him was Langridge, who played first-class cricket from 1928 to 1955, scoring over 34,000 runs, including 76 centuries. He was never picked for England, unlike his elder brother James.

Tom Pearce (Essex)

The Essex skipper either side of the Second World War, he shared the role with Denys Wilcox before the War. He was a free-scoring batsman, notching up 12,061 runs between 1929 and 1952 before becoming an England selector and, later, an international rugby referee.

Emmott Robinson (Yorkshire)

Coming to first-class cricket at 35 years young, he played for twelve years between the wars, batting in the style necessary for the needs of the side, and as a useful fast-medium bowler claiming 902 wickets. A gritty Yorkshire cricketer, he later became a first-class umpire.

Stuart Surridge (Surrey)

Of the cricket bat manufacturing family, Surridge led his county to seven successive county championships – 1952–58 – during his thirteen-year career at The Oval. He was an inspirational captain, especially in the field, but neither his batting, nor his bowling were Test-match standard.

Wilfred Wooller (Glamorgan)

A fine player for the Welsh Rugby Union side, Wooller was a true all-rounder on the oval as well as with the oval ball. In a 27-year, first-class career, he scored 13,593 runs, took 958 wickets and held 413 catches, but was never called upon by the England selectors.

Trivia

Frank Foster is the only person to have captained both England's cricket and football teams.

Pat Symcox survived being bowled by Mushtaq Ahmed at Faisalabad, because the ball failed to dislodge a bail and it rattled between his stumps.

In Western Australia, in 1894, a bowler known only as the 'Cogg' bowled a ball which was sent into a nearby tree by the batsman. The fielding side's unsuccessful attempts to retrieve the ball included climbing the tree, searching for an axe to chop it down, and shooting at it with a rifle. Efforts were abandoned after the batting team declared on 286 runs.

The first English tour of Australia in 1861–62 only came about because the author, Charles Dickens, refused an offer of a lecture tour of Australia from the sponsors, a Melbourne-based catering firm by the name of Spiers and Pond, so they turned to cricket instead.

One of the West Indies' most naturally gifted batsmen, anything that Alvin Kallicharan may have lacked in physical stature was more than made up for by his elegant range of strokes. In 66 Tests he averaged 44.43, notching twelve centuries, although, in England, he is remembered for his innings of 158 at Port of Spain in 1973–4, where he was given run out on the final ball of a day's play only to be reinstated by the umpires the following morning.

Sir Arthur Conan Doyle, the creator of Sherlock Holmes, had one first-class wicket to his name, that of W G Grace. In the match at Lord's he and W G both clean bowled each other. Dismissive of his own abilities as a writer, boxer, footballer, medical doctor and cricketer, Conan Doyle said, 'I have never specialised and have therefore been a second rater in all things.'

King George VI performed a royal hat-trick on the private ground below Windsor Castle. As Prince Albert, he dismissed the then king, Edward VII; his father, the future King George V, and his brother, the future King Edward VIII, with successive deliveries. The ball with which he achieved the feat is on display in the mess-room of the Royal Naval College at Dartmouth.